BASIC QUESTIONS OF PHILOSOPHY

Studies in Continental Thought

Martin Heidegger

BASIC QUESTIONS OF PHILOSOPHY

Selected "Problems" of "Logic"

TRANSLATED BY

Richard Rojcewicz

AND

André Schuwer

INDIANA UNIVERSITY PRESS
Bloomington & Indianapolis

Published in German as *Grundfragen der Philosophie: Ausgewählte "Probleme" der "Logik"* © 1984 by Vittorio Klostermann, Frankfurt am Main. Second edition ©1992.

The paper used in this publication meets the minimum requirements of American National Standard for Information Sciences—Permanence of Paper for Printed Library Materials, ANSI Z39.48-1984.

Manufactured in the United States of America

Library of Congress Cataloging-in-Publication Data

Heidegger, Martin, 1889-1976.
[Grundfragen der Philosophie. English]
Basic questions of philosophy : selected "problems" of "logic" / Martin Heidegger : translated by Richard Rojcewicz and André Schuwer.
p. cm. — (Studies in Continental thought)
ISBN 0-253-32685-0
1. Truth. I. Title. II. Series.
B3279.H48G7713 1994
111'.8—dc20 93-30513

1 2 3 4 5 99 98 97 96 95 94

Contents

TRANSLATORS' FOREWORD

This book is a translation of the text of Martin Heidegger's lecture course of the same title from the Winter semester 1937–1938 at the University of Freiburg. The German original appeared posthumously in 1984 (with a second edition in 1992) as volume 45 of Heidegger's "Collected Works" (*Gesamtausgabe*).

The volumes in the *Gesamtausgabe* are not appearing as critical editions. The reason is that it is their express intention to facilitate a direct contact between the reader and the work of Heidegger and to allow, as much as is possible, nothing extraneous to intervene. Thus, in particular, they include no interpretative or introductory essays. All editorial matter is kept to an absolute minimum, and there are no indexes. The words of Heidegger are reconstructed with as much faithfulness as the editor can bring to the task, and they are then simply left to speak for themselves.

It is our belief that this translation may speak for itself as well. We have on occasion felt the need to interpolate into our text Heidegger's own terminology, in order to alert the reader to some nuance we were unable to capture. For the most part, however, we have found Heidegger's language difficult to translate, to be sure, but indeed translatable, and we have endeavored to express the sense of his discourse in an English that is as fluent and natural as possible.

One word of caution: without in any way presuming to prejudge for the reader what she or he will find in these pages, we feel it incumbent on us to notify her or him that the title of the volume is, on the surface of it, something of a misnomer. For even a rather casual glance at the table of contents will show that the book does not treat the diverse topics that are ordinarily included in a text on the "Basic questions of philosophy." And indeed such a work would immediately be most un-Heideggerian, since for this philosopher there is but one basic question of philosophy and the problems of logic as we know them are only extrinsically related to it. Now the title and subtitle of this volume are in fact quite significant, although not straightforwardly so (witness the important quotation marks in the subtitle), and the theme of the book is assuredly not extraneous to Heidegger's philosophical project but lies at its very heart.

Finally, this course was delivered at the time Heidegger was composing one of his most famous posthumous texts, the currently much-discussed *Beiträge zur Philosophie* ("Contributions to philosophy"),[1] which dates from 1936–1938. The two works are intimately related, so much so that the editor of the two volumes considers the book in hand to be "the most important and immediate preparation for understanding the *Beiträge*."[2] Hence, this reason, as well as its own inherent significance, makes the present volume required study for those who would travel Heidegger's path.

R.R.
A.S.
Simon Silverman Phenomenology Center
Duquesne University

---

1. Martin Heidegger, *Beiträge zur Philosophie (Vom Ereignis)*, Frankfurt: V. Klostermann, 1989. *Gesamtausgabe* Bd. 65.

2. *Ibid.*, p. 513, "Afterword" by the editor, Friedrich-Wilhelm von Herrmann. See also the same editor's afterword to the second edition of the present volume, p. 192 below.

PREPARATORY PART

The Essence of Philosophy and the Question of Truth

Chapter One

Preliminary Interpretation of the Essence of Philosophy

§1. *Futural philosophy; restraint as the basic disposition of the relation to Being* [Seyn].

"Basic questions of philosophy"—that seems to imply there is such a thing as "philosophy" in itself, from whose domain "basic questions" could be drawn out. But such is not the case and cannot be; on the contrary, it is only the very asking of the basic questions that first determines what philosophy is. Since that is so, we need to indicate in advance how philosophy will reveal itself when we question: i.e., if we invest everything—everything without exception—in this questioning and do not merely act as if we were questioning while still believing we possess our reputed truths.

The task of this brief preliminary interpretation of the essence of philosophy will simply be to attune our questioning attitude to the right basic disposition or, to put it more prudently, to allow this basic disposition a first resonance. But, then, philosophy, the most rigorous work of abstract thought, and—disposition? Can these two really go together, philosophy and disposition? To be sure; for precisely when, and because, philosophy is the most rigorous thinking in the purest dispassion, it originates from and remains within a very high disposition. Pure dispassion is not nothing, certainly not the absence of disposition, and not the sheer coldness of the stark concept. On the contrary, the pure dispassion of thought is at bottom only the most rigorous maintenance of the highest disposition, the one open to the uniquely uncanny fact: that there *are* beings, rather than not.

If we had to say something immediately about this basic disposition *of* philosophy, i.e., of futural philosophy, we might call it "restraint" [*Verhaltenheit*]. In it, two elements originally belong together and are as one: terror in the face of what is closest and most obtrusive, namely that beings are, and awe in the face of what is remotest, namely that in beings, and before each being, Being holds sway [*das Seyn west*]. Restraint is the disposition in which this terror is not overcome and set aside but is precisely preserved and conserved through awe. Restraint is the basic disposition of the relation to Being, and in it the concealment of the essence of Being becomes what is most worthy of questioning. Only one who throws himself into the all-consuming fire of the questioning of what is most worthy of questioning has the right to say more of the basic disposition than its allusive name. Yet once he has wrested for himself this right, he will not employ it but will keep silent. For all the more reason, the basic disposition should never become an object of mere talk, for example in the popular and rash claim that what we are now teaching is a philosophy of restraint.

§2. *Philosophy as the immediately useless, though sovereign, knowledge of the essence of beings.*

Depending on the depth of the history of a people, there will exist or will not exist, in the all-determining beginning, the poetizing of the poet and the thinking of the thinker, i.e., philosophy. A historical people without philosophy is like an eagle without the high expanse of the radiant aether, where its flight reaches the purest soaring.

Philosophy is completely different from "world-view" and is fundamentally distinct from all "science." Philosophy cannot by itself replace either world-view or science; nor can it ever be appreciated by them. Philosophy cannot at all be measured by anything else but only by its own now shining, now hidden, essence. If we attempt to calculate whether philosophy has any immediate use and what that use might be, we will find that philosophy accomplishes nothing.

It belongs necessarily to the character of ordinary opinion and "practical" thinking always to misjudge philosophy, whether by overestimating or underestimating it. Philosophy is overestimated if one expects its thinking to have an immediately useful effect. Philosophy is underestimated if one finds in its concepts merely abstract (remote and watered down) representations of things that have already been solidly secured in experience.

Yet genuine philosophical knowledge is never the mere addition of the most general representations, limping behind a being already known anyway. Philosophy is rather the reverse, a knowledge that leaps ahead, opening up new domains of questioning and aspects of questioning about the essence of things, an essence that constantly conceals itself anew. That is precisely the reason this knowledge can never be made useful. Philosophical reflection has an effect, if it does, always only mediately, by making available new aspects for all comportment and new principles for all decisions. But philosophy has this power only when it risks what is most proper to it, namely to posit in a thoughtful way for the existence of man [*das Dasein des Menschen*] the goal of all reflection and to establish thereby in the history of man a hidden sovereignty. We must therefore say philosophy is the immediately useless, though sovereign, knowledge of the essence of things.

The essence of beings, however, is always the most worthy of questioning. Insofar as philosophy, in its incessant questioning, merely struggles to appreciate what is most worthy of questioning and apparently never yields results, it will always and necessarily seem strange to a thinking preoccupied with calculation, use, and ease of learning. The sciences, and indeed not only the natural sciences, must strive increasingly and, it seems, irresistibly for a complete "technologizing" in order to proceed to the end of their course, laid down for them so long ago. At the same time, the sciences appear to possess genuine knowledge. For these reasons, the sharpest possible alienation with regard to philosophy and at the same time a presumed convincing proof of the futility of philosophy occur in and through the sciences.

(*Truth and "science"*: if, and only if, we believe ourselves to be in possession of the "truth," do we have science and its business. Yet science is the disavowal of all knowledge of truth. To hold that today science meets with hostility is a basic error: never has science fared better than it does today, and it will fare still better in the future. But no one who knows will envy scientists—the most miserable slaves of modern times.)

(The withdrawal of science into what is worthy of questioning [Cf. "The Self-Determination of the German University"] is the dissolution of modern science.)

§3. *Questioning the truth of Being, as sovereign knowledge.*

Philosophy is the useless though sovereign knowledge of the essence of beings. The sovereignty is based on the goal established by thinking for all reflection. But what goal does our thinking posit? The positing of the goal for all reflection possesses truth only where and when such a goal is sought. When we Germans seek this goal, and as long as we do so, we have also already found it. For *our goal is the very seeking itself*. What else is the seeking but the most constant being-in-proximity to what conceals itself, out of which each need happens to come to us and every jubilation fills us with enthusiasm. The very seeking is the goal and at the same time what is found.

Obvious misgivings now arise. If seeking is supposed to be the goal, then is not what is established as a goal actually the limitless absence of any goal? This is the way calculating reason thinks. If seeking is supposed to be the very goal, then do not restlessness and dissatisfaction become perpetuated? This is the opinion of the feeling that is avid for quick possessions. Yet we maintain that seeking brings into existence the highest constancy and equanimity—though only when this seeking *genuinely* seeks, i.e., extends into the farthest reaches of what is most concealed and thereby leaves behind all mere curiosity. And what is more concealed than the ground of what is so uncanny, namely that beings are rather than are not? What withdraws from us more than the essence of Being, i.e., the essence of that which, in all the fabricated and disposed beings holding sway around us and bearing us on, is the closest but at the same time the most worn out (through constant handling) and therefore the most ungraspable?

To posit the very seeking as a goal means to anchor the beginning and the end of all reflection in the question of the truth—not of this or that being or even of all beings, but of Being itself. The grandeur of man is measured according to what he seeks and according to the urgency by which he remains a seeker.

Such questioning of the truth of Being is sovereign knowledge, philosophy. Here questioning already counts as knowing, because no matter how essential and decisive an answer might be, the answer cannot be other than the penultimate step in the long series of steps of a questioning founded in itself. In the domain of genuine seeking, to find does not mean to cease seeking but is the highest intensity of seeking.

This preliminary interpretation of the essence of philosophy will, to be sure, have meaning for us only when we experience such knowledge in the labor of questioning—therefore "Basic questions of philosophy." But which question will we raise?

Chapter Two

The Question of Truth as a Basic Question[1]

§4. *Truth as a "problem" of "logic" (correctness of an assertion) distorts every view of the essence of truth.*

The two titles announce the task of our lectures in a double way, though without making it clear what the content of the discussions is to be. To learn that, let us take the subtitle as our point of departure. Accordingly, the course will be about logic. Traditionally, this is a "discipline," a branch of philosophy, supposing that philosophy itself is taken as a discipline, which scholasticism divides into individual branches: logic, ethics, aesthetics, etc., each of which then encompasses a series of concomitant "problems." "Problems"—the word in quotation marks serves to name questions that are no longer truly asked. They have been frozen as questions, and it is only a matter of finding the answer or, rather, modifying answers already found, collating previous opinions and reconciling them. Such "problems" are therefore particularly prone to conceal genuine questions and to dismiss out of hand, as too strange, certain questions that have never yet been raised, indeed to misinterpret completely the essence of questioning. The so-called "problems" can thus readily usurp the place of the basic questions of philosophy. Such "problems" of

1. The question of the essence of truth is the casting of the one and only goal which by itself reaches out beyond itself, truth understood here as the truth of Being, seen in terms of the essence of the appropriating event [*vom Wesen des Ereignisses*]. What is at stake is not only the removal of goal-lessness but, above all, the overcoming of the resistance against any search for a goal.

philosophic learnedness then have, from the standpoint of genuine philosophy, this remarkable distinction that, under the impressive appearance of "problems," they may summarily and decisively prevent real questioning.

What we intend to discuss here is just such a "problem" of "logic." But that means we shall endeavor to go forthwith beyond the "problem," the frozen question, and likewise beyond "logic" as a discipline of scholastically degenerated philosophical learnedness, to a philosophical questioning that is basic, that penetrates into the ground. Yet we shall have to make the "problems" our point of departure, for only in this way can we see the traditional form of the question, which we shall put into question, but which also still rules us. Because what is traditional often has behind itself a very long past, it is not something arbitrary but harbors in itself still the trace of an erstwhile genuine necessity. To be sure, such traces can only be seen once the traditional is set back upon its ground.

We shall select a "problem of logic" behind which lies hidden a still unasked "basic question of philosophy." "Logic" is our abbreviated expression for λογικὴ ἐπιστήμη. That means "knowledge about λόγος," understood as assertion. To what extent is assertion the theme of logic? And how does the construction of this "branch" of philosophy result from it? Let us clarify this briefly so that the name "logic" does not remain an empty title.

What provides the assertion—a statement of the kind, "The stone is hard," "The sky is covered"—such a rank that it is made explicitly the object of a branch of knowledge, namely, logic? The assertion asserts something about a being, that it is and how it is. In doing so, the assertion is directed to [*richten auf*] the being, and if the assertion in its very asserting conforms to [*sich richten nach*] the being, and if what it asserts maintains this direction [*Richtung*] and on that basis represents the being, then the assertion is correct [*richtig*]. The correctness of an assertion—that means for us, and has meant from time immemorial, truth. The assertion is hence the seat and place of truth—but also of untruth, falsity and lies. The assertion is the basic form of those utterances that can be either true or false. It is not as a kind of utterance and not as a verbal structure, but as the seat and place of correctness, i.e., of truth, that the assertion, the λόγος, is an eminent "object" of knowledge. Then again, as this place of truth, it claims special attention only because the truth and the possession of the truth attract exceptional interest. We seek the truth, we speak of the "will to truth," we believe we possess the truth, we prize the "value" of the truth. The truth and its possession, or non-possession, are what make us uneasy, happy, or disappointed, and only for that reason does the assertion, as the place of truth, receive basically a special attention, and furthermore, only for that reason is there basically something like "logic." I intentionally use the word "basically," since matters have been quite different for a long time now, and the situation has been precisely the opposite. For a long time there has been logic as a discipline of scholastic philosophy, and in fact precisely since the beginning of Plato's school, but indeed only since then. Because logic exists as the examination of λόγος, there is also the "problem" of "truth," truth taken as the distinctive property of λόγος. The "problem of truth" is therefore a problem of "logic" or, as we say in more modern times, theory of knowledge. Truth is that "value" by which knowledge first counts as knowledge. And the basic form of knowledge is the judgment, the proposition, the assertion, the λόγος. Theory of knowledge is therefore always "logic" in the just-mentioned essential sense.

Even though it might sound exaggerated to say that the problem of truth exists as a "problem" because there is "logic" and because this discipline is from time to time taken up once again and presented under a new veneer, nevertheless it remains undebatable that since the time of Plato and Aristotle the question of truth has been a question of logic. This implies that the search for what truth is moves along the paths and in the perspectives which were firmly laid down by the approach and the range of tasks of logic and its presuppositions. To mention only more modern thinkers, this fact can easily be substantiated on the basis of the works of Kant, Hegel, and Nietzsche. Though it is certain that for these philosophers and in general for the entire tradition of Western philosophy, the question of truth is a meditation on thinking and λόγος, and hence is a question of "logic," yet it would be completely superficial and falsifying to claim that these thinkers have raised the question of truth, and consequently sought an answer to it, *only* because logic exists and logic insists on such a question. Presumably the concern that led these thinkers to the question of truth was not merely the one of improving and reforming logic but precisely that "interest" every man has in the truth, man as one who is exposed to beings and thus is himself a being.

Nevertheless it may be that this "interest" in truth, which can be alive even where there is no "interest" in "logic," can, in the course of time, still be forced by the domination of logic into a quite definite direction and stamped with a wholly determined form. That is in fact how matters stand. Even where the question of truth does not stem from an interest in logic, the treatment of the question still moves in the paths of logic.

In brief, then, from time immemorial truth has been a "problem of logic" but not a basic question of philosophy.

This fact even bears on Nietzsche, and in the sharpest way, i.e., precisely where the question of truth was especially raised in Occidental philosophy in the most passionate manner. For Nietzsche's starting point is that we do not possess the "truth," which obviously makes the question of truth most imperative; secondly, he asks what truth might be worth; thirdly, he questions the origin of the "will to truth." And yet, in spite of this radicalism of questioning, apparently never to be surpassed, the question of truth remains caught, even for Nietzsche, in the trammels of "logic."

What is so wrong with that? For one, it could be that the perspective of all logic as logic precisely distorts every view of the essence of truth. It could be that the presuppositions of all logic do not permit an original questioning of truth. It could be that logic does not even attain the portico of the question of truth.

These remarks at least suggest that the "problem of truth" stands within a long tradition which has increasingly removed the *question* of truth from its root and ground and indeed that the question of truth has never yet been raised originally. Insofar as modern and contemporary thought moves wholly within the perspectives of this tradition, an original questioning of truth becomes accessible only with difficulty, indeed must appear strange, if not downright foolish.

§5. *Discussion of truth by asking the basic question of philosophy, including a historical confrontation with Western philosophy. The need and the necessity of an original questioning.*

If, in what follows, we are not to discuss truth as a "problem of logic" but instead are to question it while asking the basic question of philosophy, then at the very outset we will need to take into account these difficulties of understanding, i.e., we will have to recognize that today the question of truth involves a confrontation with the whole of Western philosophy and can never be broached without this historical confrontation. A historical [*geschichtlich*] confrontation, however, is essentially different from a *historiographical* [*historisch*] reckoning of and acquaintance with the past. What a historical confrontation means should become clear in actually thinking through the question of truth.

The question of truth—even if the answer is not yet forthcoming—already sounds, merely as a question, very presumptuous. For if behind such questioning there did not lie the claim to indeed know the truth itself in some sort of way, then all this to-do would be a mere game. And yet greater than this claim is the holding back to which the question of truth must be attuned. For it is not a matter of taking up again a well-established "problem;" on the contrary, the question of truth is to be raised as a basic question. That means truth must first be esteemed as basically worthy of questioning, that is, worthy of questioning in its ground. Whoever holds himself in this attitude, as esteeming something higher, will be free of all presumption. Nevertheless, seen from the outside, the question of truth always retains the appearance of arrogance: to want to decide what is primary and what is ultimate. Here only the correct questioning itself and the experience of its necessity can forge the appropriate attitude.

But in view of the tradition preserved throughout two millennia, how are we supposed to experience the necessity of an original questioning, and of a stepping out of the circuit of the traditional problem of truth, and consequently the need of an other sort of questioning? Why can we not and should we not adhere to "the old"; why does the determination of truth hitherto not satisfy us? The answer to these questions is already nothing less than a return into the more original essence of truth, which indeed must first be put on its way by our very questioning. Similarly, we can already convince ourselves by a simple reflection on the traditional concept of truth that here we have in hand something worthy of questioning which has remained unquestioned.

RECAPITULATION

1) The question of truth as the most necessary philosophical question in an age that is totally unquestioning.

If we try to determine the present situation of man on earth metaphysically—thus not historiographically and not in terms of world-view—then it must be said that man is beginning to enter the age of the total unquestionableness of all things and of all contrivances. That is truly an uncanny occurrence, whose orientation no one can establish and whose bearing no one can evaluate.

Only one thing is immediately clear: in this completely unquestioning age, philosophy, as the questioning that calls forth what is most worthy of questioning, becomes inevitably most strange. Therefore it is the most necessary. And necessity has its most powerful form in the simple. The simple, however, is our name for what is inconspicuously the most difficult, which, when it occurs, appears to everyone immediately and ever again as the easiest and most accessible; yet it remains incontestably the most difficult. The simple is the most difficult, for the multiple admits and favors dispersion, and all dispersion, as a counter-reaction to the unification of man in his constant flight from himself—i.e., from his relation to Being itself—confirms and thereby alleviates and releases the heavy burden of existence. The multiple is the easy—even where concern over it seems toilsome. For progress from one thing to another is always a relaxation, and it is precisely this progress that is not allowed by the simple, which presses on instead to a constant return to the same in a constant self-enrichment. Only if we risk the simple do we arrive within the arena of the necessary. What is most necessary in philosophy—supposing that it must again become the strangest—is precisely that simple question by which it, in its questioning, is first brought to itself: namely, the question of truth.

2) What is worthy of questioning in the determination of truth hitherto (truth as the correctness of an assertion) as compelling us toward the question of truth.

The question of truth, as it has been treated hitherto, is a "problem of logic." If from this "problem"—i.e., from the moribund question—a living question is to arise, and if this is not to be arbitrary and artificial, but necessary in an original way, then we have to strive for a genuine experience of what is compelling us toward the question of truth.

The determination of truth up to now, and still valid everywhere in the most varied trappings, runs as follows: truth is the correctness of a representation of a being. All representing of beings is a predicating about them, although this predication can be accomplished silently and does not need to be pronounced. The most common form of predication is the assertion, the simple proposition, the λόγος, and therefore the correctness of representation—truth—is to be found there in the most immediate way. Truth has its place and seat in λόγος. The more precise determination of truth then becomes the task of a meditation on λόγος, a task of "logic."

What can now compel us to turn the usual definition of truth as correctness of representation into a question? This can indeed only be the circumstance, perhaps still hidden, that the unquestioned determination of truth as correctness contains something worthy of questioning which by itself requires being put into question. It could be objected that not everything questionable needs to be made the object of a question. Perhaps; therefore we want to examine whether and to what extent there is in the usual determination of truth as correctness something worthy of questioning in the first place, and whether, furthermore, it is of such a kind that we cannot pass over it unheeded and unquestioned—supposing that we claim to be informed about the truth, in accord with others and with ourselves.

§6. *The traditional determination of truth as correctness.*

We say that an assertion, or the knowledge embedded in it, is true insofar as it conforms to [*sich richten nach*] its object. Truth is correctness [*Richtigkeit*]. In the early modern age, though above all in medieval times, this *rectitudo* was also called *adaequatio* (adequation), *assimilatio* (assimilation), or *convenientia* (correspondence). These determinations revert back to Aristotle, with whom the great Greek philosophy comes to its end. Aristotle conceives of truth, which has its home in λόγος (assertion), as ὁμοίωσις (assimilation). The representation (νόημα) is assimilated to what is to be grasped. The representational assertion about the hard stone, or representation in general, is of course something pertaining to the "soul" (ψυχή), something "spiritual." At any event, it is not of the type of the stone. Then how is the representation supposed to assimilate itself to the stone? The representation is not supposed to, and cannot, become stone-like, nor should it, in the corresponding case of an assertion about the table, become woody, or in representing a stream become liquid. Nevertheless, the representation must make itself similar to the being at hand: i.e., as representing [*Vor-stellen*], it must posit the encountered before us [*vor uns hin-stellen*] and maintain it as so posited. The re-presenting, the positing-before (i.e., the thinking), conforms to the being so as to let it appear in the assertion as it is.

The relation of a representation to an object (ἀντικείμενον) is the most "natural" thing in the world, so much so that we are almost ashamed to still speak explicitly of it. Therefore, the naive view, not yet tainted by "epistemology," will not be able to see what is supposed to be incorrect or even merely questionable in the determination of truth as correctness. Admittedly, throughout the many endeavors of man to attain a knowledge of beings, it often happens unfortunately that we do not grasp beings as they are and are deluded about them. But even delusion occurs only where the intention prevails of conforming to beings. We can delude others and take them in only if the others, just as we ourselves, are in advance in an attitude of conforming to beings and aiming at correctness. Correctness is the standard and the measure even for incorrectness. Thus the determination of truth as correctness, together with its counterpart, namely incorrectness (falsity), is in fact clear as day. Because this conception of truth emerges, as is obvious, entirely from the "natural" way of thinking, and corresponds to it, it has lasted throughout the centuries and has long ago been hardened into something taken for granted.

Truth is correctness, or in the more usual formula: truth is the correspondence of knowledge (representation, thought, judgment, assertion) with the object.

→ *Truth*
correctness
rectitudo
adaequatio
assimilatio
convenientia
ὁμοίωσις
→ *correspondence*

§7. *The controversy between idealism and realism on the common soil of a conception of truth as the correctness of a representation.*

To be sure, in the course of time objections arose against this conception of truth. These objections were based, specifically, on doubt as to whether our representations reached the being itself in itself at all and did not rather remain enclosed within the circuit of their own activity, hence in the realm of the "soul," the "spirit," "consciousness," the "ego." Surrender to this doubt leads to the view that what we attain in our representing is always only something re-presented by us, hence is itself a representation. Consequently knowledge and assertions consist in the representation of representations and hence in a combination of representations. This combining is an activity and a process taking place merely "in our consciousness." The adherents of this doctrine believe they have "critically" purified and surpassed the usual determination of truth as correctness. But this "belief" is mistaken. The doctrine that knowledge relates only to representations (the represented) merely restricts the reach of a representation; yet it still claims that this restricted representation conforms to the represented and *only* to the represented. Thus even here a standard or measure is presupposed, to which the representing conforms. Even here truth is conceived as correctness.

The doctrine that our representations relate *only* to the represented, the *perceptum*, the *idea*, is called idealism. The counterclaim, according to which our representations reach the things themselves (*res*) and what belongs to them (*realia*), has been called, ever since the advance of idealism, realism. Thus these hostile brothers, each of whom likes to think himself superior to the other, are unwittingly in complete accord with regard to the essence, i.e., with regard to what provides the presupposition and the very possibility of their controversy: that the relation to beings is a representing of them and that the truth of the representation consists in its correctness. A thinker such as Kant, who founded idealism and strictly adhered to it, and who has most profoundly thought it through, concedes in advance that the conception of truth as correctness of a representation—as correspondence with the object—is inviolable. Realism, for its part, is captive to a great error when it claims that even Kant, the most profound "idealist," is a witness for the defense of realism. On the contrary, the consequence of Kant's adherence to the traditional determination of truth as correctness is simply the opposite, namely that realism, in its determination of truth as correctness of a representation, stands on the same ground as idealism, and is even itself idealism, according to a more rigorous and more original concept of "idealism." For even according to the doctrine of realism—the critical and the naive—the *res*, beings, are attained by means of the representation, the *idea*. Idealism and realism therefore comprise the two most extreme basic positions as regards the relation of man to beings. All past theories concerning this relation and its character—truth as correctness—are either one-sided caricatures of the extreme positions or diverse variations on the numerous mixtures and distortions of the two doctrines. The controversy among all these opinions can still go on endlessly, without ever leading to genuine reflection or to an insight, because it is characteristic of this sterile wrangling to renounce in advance the question of the soil upon which the combatants stand. In other words, the conception of truth as correctness of representation is taken for granted everywhere, in philosophy just as in extra-philosophical opinion.

The more obvious and the more unquestioned the usual determination of truth, the simpler has to be what is worthy of question in this determination, supposing something of the sort is indeed concealed therein. Yet the more simple what is worthy of questioning proves to be, the more difficult it will be to grasp this simple in its inner fullness, i.e., to grasp it simply and unitarily as what is worthy of question, i.e., perplexing, and to adhere to it in order to unfold its proper essence and thus pose it back upon its hidden ground.

§8. *The space of the fourfold-unitary openness. First directive toward what is worthy of questioning in the traditional determination of truth as correctness.*

We must now seek a first directive toward what is worthy of questioning here, in order to secure our questioning in general and, even if only preliminarily, assure ourselves of its legitimacy. Let us reflect: if our representations and assertions—e.g., the statement, "The stone is hard"—are supposed to conform to the object, then this being, the stone itself, must be accessible in advance: in order to present itself as a standard and measure for the conformity with it. In short, the being, in this case the thing, must be out in the open. Even more: not only must the stone itself—in order to remain with our example—be out in the open but so must the domain which the conformity with the thing has to traverse in order to read off from it, in the mode of representing, what characterizes the being in its being thus and so. Moreover, the human who is representing, and who in his representing conforms to the thing, must also be open. He must be open for what encounters him, so that it might encounter him. Finally, the person must also be open to his fellows, so that, co-representing what is communicated to him in their assertions, he can, together with the others and out of a being-with them, conform to the same thing and be in agreement with them about the correctness of the representing.

In the correctness of the representational assertion there holds sway consequently a four-fold openness: (1) of the thing,

(2) of the region between thing and man, (3) of man himself with regard to the thing, and (4) of man to fellow man.

This four-fold openness would not be what it is and what it has to be if each of these opennesses were separately encapsulated from the others. This four-fold openness holds sway rather as one and unitary, and in its compass every conformity to . . . and every correctness and incorrectness of representing come into play and maintain themselves. If we attend to this multiple and yet unitary openness then with one stroke we find ourselves transported into another realm beyond correctness and its concomitant representational activity.

This multiple-unitary openness holds sway *in* correctness. The openness is not first produced by the correctness of the representing, but rather, just the reverse, it is taken over as what was always already holding sway. Correctness of representation is only possible if it can establish itself in this openness which supports it and vaults it over. The openness is the ground and the soil and the arena of all correctness. Thus as long as truth is conceived as correctness, and correctness itself passes unquestioned, i.e., as something ultimate and primary, this conception of truth—no matter how long a tradition has again and again confirmed it—remains groundless. But, as soon as that openness, as the possibility and the ground of correctness, comes into view, even if unclearly, truth conceived as correctness becomes questionable.

§9. *The conception of truth and of the essence of man. The basic question of truth.*

a) The determination of the essence of truth as connected to the determination of the essence of man.

We might marvel that up to now the ground of correctness has never been seriously put into question. But this omission proves to be less peculiar if we consider that the relation of man to beings, understood from time immemorial as immediate representing and perceiving, seems to be the most ordinary aspect of human experience and therefore the most obvious. The domination of this relation of man to beings soon became so insistent that even the very essence of man was determined in reference to it. For what is the meaning of the ancient, and still currently valid, definition of the essence of man: *animal rationale* (ζῷον λόγον ἔχον)? This determination is translated, i.e., interpreted, as follows: man is the rational living being; man is an animal, but one endowed with reason. What does reason, *ratio*, νοῦς, mean? If we think metaphysically, as is necessary here, and not psychologically, then reason means the immediate perception of beings. The familiar definition of man now has an altogether different ring: man—the being that perceives beings. Here we touch upon an important, though still unclear, connection: the familiarity of the conception of truth as correctness is as old as the familiarity of that definition of the essence of man, and consequently the determination of the essence of truth depends on what happens to be the determination of the essence of man. Or should we not maintain the reverse, that the conception of the essence of man depends upon the way truth is understood at any particular time?

b) The question of the ground of the possibility of all correctness as the basic question of truth.

We are not yet in a position to decide that question. At the moment it is enough for us to glimpse something worthy of questioning in the familiar theory of truth as correctness. This questionable element is again of such a kind that it must be recognized and displayed as the ground of the possibility of all correctness. If we interrogate this ground or *basis* of correctness, then we are asking about truth in the sense of a *basic* question. It is therefore not a matter of arbitrariness, and still less an empty passion, to revise, no matter the cost, what has come down to us, i.e., to take the traditional theory of truth as correctness ultimately for granted no longer, but to experience it instead as a source of uneasiness.

But the reference to *openness* as the ground of correctness is still quite extrinsic: it can only intimate, in a very preliminary way, that and to what extent something worthy of questioning lies hidden in the traditional theory of truth.

What really is the ground of correctness, and where and how does this multiple and yet unitary openness have its own essence and content—all these things remain in the dark. Therefore we cannot explain why this ground is so rarely glimpsed, and then only from afar. We cannot even begin to estimate what will happen to man when the experience of this ground is brought to bear in its full scope.

What we need to discuss above all, however, is why and wherefore we are raising the question that we are, since the familiar conception of truth has satisfied two thousand years of Western history.

RECAPITULATION

1) The relation between question and answer in the domain of philosophy.

These lectures are proclaiming no eternal truths. I say this to obviate misunderstandings which could easily impede our collaboration. I am not capable of such a proclamation, nor is it my task. Rather, what is at issue here is questioning, the exercise of right questioning, to be achieved in the actual performance of it. This seems to be little enough for one who is pressing on to the possession of answers. But in philosophy the relation of question and answer is quite peculiar. To speak metaphorically, it is like climbing a mountain. We will get nowhere by positioning ourselves on the plane of ordinary opinion and merely talking about the mountain, in order to gain in that way a "lived experience" of it. No, the climbing and the approach to the peak succeed only if we begin to mount. The peak might indeed be lost from view as we climb, and yet we keep coming closer to it. Furthermore, climbing includes slipping and sliding back and, in philosophy, even falling. Only one who is truly climbing can fall down. What if those who fall down experience the peak, the mountain, and its *height* most profoundly, more profoundly and more uniquely than the ones who apparently reach the top, which for them soon loses its height and becomes a plane and something habitual? It is not possible to judge and measure either philosophy, or art, or, in general, any creative dealing with beings, with the aid of the facile bureaucracy of sound common sense and a presumably healthy "instinct" (already distorted and misled long ago), no more than with the empty sagacity of a so-called intellectual. Here the whole and every single thing within it can be experienced only in the actual performance of the painful work of climbing.

Anyone here who is only snatching up isolated propositions is not climbing along with me. The task is to go along every single step and the whole series of steps. Only in that way will there be a disclosure of the matter we are meditating on and of the goal we want to reach.

2) The customary determination of truth as correctness of representation, and the fourfold-unitary openness as the question-worthy ground of the possibility of the correctness of representation.

We are asking the question of truth. The customary determination of truth runs: truth is the correctness of a representation, the correspondence of an assertion (a proposition) with a thing. Although in the course of the history of Western thinking, various opinions about knowledge and representation have arisen and have again and again debated each other and intermingled with each other, yet the same conception of truth as correctness of representation remains the standard. The two main theories of knowledge and representation, idealism and realism, are not distinct with regard to their conception of truth: they are alike in taking truth to be a determination of a representation, of an assertion. They are distinct only with regard to their views about the reach of the representing: either the representation attains the things themselves—*res, realia*—(realism), or the representation always remains related merely to the represented as such—*perceptum, idea*—(idealism). Thus in spite of the apparent difference of logical and epistemological standpoints, there is an overarching and ruling agreement over what truth is: correctness of representing.

But in this self-evident determination of truth as correctness there lurks something worthy of questioning: that multiple-unitary openness of the things, of the region between things and man, of man himself, and of man to fellow man. If it were not for this openness, there could never occur a representing that conforms to a thing. For this conforming to . . . does not first create the openness of the things and the openness of man for what he might encounter. On the contrary, it settles into an openness already holding sway and does so, as it were, each time anew. This openness is therefore the ground of the possibility of correctness and as this ground it is something worthy of questioning and inquiry. At first it is unclear what it really is that we are referring to here and are calling openness. And that could only be one more reason to abandon the inquiry into what we say is worthy of questioning, especially if we recall that for two thousand years Western history has been satisfied with the ordinary conception of truth.

c) The question of truth as the most questionable of our previous history and the most worthy of questioning of our future history.

At this hour in the history of the world we can and must ask where the Occident has finally arrived with its conception of truth. Where do we stand today? What and where is truth? In spite of everything correct, have we lost the truth? Has the West not fallen into a situation where all goals are dubious and where all bustle and bother merely aim at finding a means of escape? How else are we supposed to understand *metaphysically* that Western man is driven either to the complete destruction of what has been handed down or to warding off this destruction?

These means of escape are not decisions. Extreme decisions require the positing of goals that transcend all usefulness and every purpose and therefore are alone powerful enough to instigate a new creating and founding. Decisions, as such positing of goals, especially in the situation we sketched, need the grounding of the soil and the installation of the perspective with regard to which and in which they are supposed to be made.

Are we—and for that decision this is most decisive—are we willfully and knowingly only at what lies closest, i.e., at the *preparation* for this decision?

In light of the task, is the question of truth only a "problem of logic," or is the question of truth the most questionable one of our past history and the most worthy of questioning of our future history? For everyone who has eyes to see, and especially for everyone who has torn himself from the indolence of an uncreative adherence to the past—e.g., Christianity—and from the presumption to possess the remedy, for everyone who does not want to go back but to go forward, not toward "progress" but into the concealed future, for such ones the task is decided. It requires *reflection* as the first and the most constant and the ultimate. With the question of truth—raised as it were in an "academic" lecture—we shall attempt to take some steps in such reflection.

Now, since the most preliminary questioning about truth has been confused long ago, thrown off the track and deprived of direction, we must reflect first of all on what is foundational with regard to the question of truth.

MAIN PART

Foundational Issues in the Question of Truth

Chapter One

The Basic Question of the Essence of Truth as a Historical Reflection

§10. *The ambiguity of the question of truth: the search for what is true—reflection on the essence of truth.*

Let us begin with a simple reflection. It will lead into a *historical* reflection, and this in turn will allow the unfolding of the question of truth to become a reflection on its necessity and its unique character.

The question of truth asks about "truth." The question is so straightforward that foundational deliberations regarding the question of truth might appear superfluous. To raise the question of truth surely means to seek the truth. And that means to seek what is true, or, according to what has been clarified above, to establish and ascertain what is correct about things and about all beings, whereby the correct is to be understood primarily in the sense of aims and standards to which all our actions and behavior conform. To raise the question of "truth" means to seek the true.

But "the true," here being sought, certainly signifies more than just any correct statements about any objects whatever. We are seeking more than mere particular instructions for correct action. The true to which we give that name, and which we perhaps more desire than seek, also does not mean merely the sum of *all* correct statements and instructions for correct action. To seek the true means to pursue what is correct in the sense of that to which all commission and omission and all judgments about things are connected in advance, that to which our historical humanity is attached. The true means for us here that for which we live and die. *This* true is "truth."

Already from these brief reflections we can infer that the word "truth" is not univocal. It means the true, first of all whatever is at any given time correct in knowledge and in action and disposition, and then, more emphatically, that upon which everything depends and from which everything is ruled and decided.

But even if we heed this plurivocity, in the context of speaking about the true and truth, we can nevertheless claim, and indeed rightfully, that in this seeking of the true—even if we mean what is decisively true—we are still not yet raising the question of truth: that is, insofar as we consider truth that which makes something true true and determines every single true thing to be the true thing it is. Just as cleverness is what distinguishes all clever people as such, so truth, rigorously thought, means what determines all that is true to be so. For ages, that which universally determines every individual thing has been called the essence. Through it, anything and everything is delimited in what it is and is delineated against other things. Truth means nothing but the essence of the true. Truth comprises that which distinguishes something true as such, just as speed indicates what determines speedy things as such. Thus to raise the question of truth does not mean to seek *a* true or *the* true but to seek the essence, i.e., to define the universal properties of whatever is true. Thereby we encounter for the first time the decisive ambiguity in talk of the "question of truth."

§11. *The question of truth as a question of the essence of the true: not an inquiry into the universal concept of the true.*

To raise the question of truth can mean: (1) to seek the true, (2) to delimit the essence of everything true. It is easy to discover which of these two ways of raising the question of truth is the more urgent and the more important. Obviously, it is the search for the true and above all in the sense of the true that rules and decides everything. In comparison, it appears that the question of truth, i.e., of the essence of the true, is something merely supplementary, nay, even superfluous. For the essence in the sense of the universal which applies in each case to the many particulars, as, e.g., the universal representation "house" applies to all real and possible houses, this universal is grasped and formulated in a concept. To think the mere concept of something is precisely to abstract from particular realities. Thus if we desire the true and seek it, we will not strive for truth in the sense of the mere concept, to which anything true as true is subordinated. When we seek the true, we want to gain possession of that upon which our historical humanity is posited and by which it is thoroughly dominated and through which it is raised above itself. Every genuine attitude of man, who dwells in the real and wants to transform what is real, remove it from its place and liberate it to higher possibilities, will arrive at the univocal demand that can be expressed briefly as follows: we desire what is true, why should we be concerned with truth itself?

But insofar as we are here inquiring *philosophically*, and philosophy is the knowledge of the essence of things, we already have decided otherwise. In philosophizing, we reflect on the *essence* of the true, we abide by that which is precisely not a concern for ones who desire the true. And hence they, who desire the true, must reject our intention as something extrinsic and useless. It was not in vain, but rather in anticipation of this rejection of our proposal, that at the very outset we said philosophy is immediately useless knowledge. Our reflection on correctness and on truth itself can accomplish nothing toward the correct solution of economic difficulties, or toward the correct improvement and assurance of the public health, nor can it contribute anything to the correct increase of the speed of airplanes, or to the correct improvement of radio reception, and likewise just as little to the correct design of instructional projects in the schools. With regard to all these urgent matters of daily life, philosophy fails. Nay, even more: because it inquires only into the essence of truth and does not determine individual truths, philosophy will not be able to settle anything about the decisively true. Philosophy is immediately useless knowledge and yet still something else: sovereign knowledge.

If that is so, then knowledge of the essence of the true, i.e., knowledge of the truth, could perhaps still bear a significance and even one that reaches beyond everything useful. But how is the essence, as a universal concept, supposed to acquire a sovereign rank? What is more shadowy, and therefore more impotent, than a mere concept?

In this regard a question still remains, one that is perhaps most intimately connected to the question of truth as the question of the essence of the true. Have we determined the essence sufficiently in identifying it with the concept? Perhaps the essence of the true, hence truth itself, is not grasped at all if we merely represent in general that which applies universally to everything true as such. Perhaps the essence of the true, hence truth itself, is not what applies indifferently with regard to the true but is the most essential truth. In that case, the genuine and decisive truth, upon which everything must be posited, would be precisely this *essence* of the true, the truth itself. In that case, the standpoint which pretends to care so much about reality—"We desire the true, why should we be concerned with truth itself?"—would be a great error, the error of errors, and up to now the most enduring of all errors. Supposing truth is this truth, then our inquiry into truth as the question of the essence of all truths, provided we carry it out correctly, will not be mere play with empty concepts.

§12. *The question of the legitimacy of the ordinary determination of truth, as point of departure for a return to the ground of the possibility of correctness.*

The fact that we are immediately leaving behind the customary conception of truth and are trying to attain the ground upon which the determination of truth as correctness is founded shows that we are not entangled in an empty squabble about the mere definition of the concept of truth but that we want to touch something essential. Through such a return to the ground—to what is worthy of questioning—we put into question the determination of truth hitherto and in so doing make ourselves free of it.

But do we really make ourselves free? Are we not binding ourselves all the more to this essential definition, to such an extent that it becomes the obligatory one? Let us not deceive ourselves.

With the return to that openness by which all correctness first becomes possible, we in fact presuppose that the determination of truth as correctness has indeed its own legitimacy. Is this then already proved? The characterization of truth as correctness could very well be an error. At any rate, up to now it has not been shown that this characterization is *not* an error. But if the conception of truth as correctness is an error, what then about the positing of the ground of the possibility of correctness? To say the least, such a positing can in that case not claim to grasp the essence of truth more fundamentally. On the contrary, we must concede that what supports an error and founds it is a fortiori erroneous.

What is the meaning of the return to the manifold-unitary openness if it is not proven in advance that what we take to be the point of departure for the return, namely the ordinary determination of truth as correctness, has its own justification?

Now, in fact, the conception of truth as correctness is confirmed through a long tradition. But the appeal to tradition is not yet a foundation and safeguard of the truth of an intuition. For centuries, the tradition clung to the opinion that the sun revolves around the earth, and the eyes themselves even confirmed it. Nevertheless, this opinion could be shaken. Perhaps the traditional character of an insight is even an objection against its correctness. Is it not possible that what might in itself be an error can become a "truth" by being believed long enough? Whatever may be the case here, the mere long duration and venerable character of a tradition are not, by themselves, a reliable ground to prove the truth of an essential determination.

But must we appeal to traditional opinions in order to ascertain the legitimacy of the determination of truth as correctness? After all, we can form for ourselves a judgment about this legitimacy. And that is not difficult, for the characterization of truth as the correspondence of a representation with an object is self-evident. This obviousness has the advantage that it is relieved from further foundation. What we call the obvious is what is clearly evident on its own, without further thought. Now, to be sure, it has been shown conclusively enough that if we take truth as correctness of representation, we in fact avoid further thought and that here something is evident for us because we are renouncing every attempt to elucidate it more closely and more genuinely. What kind of obviousness is it, however, which subsists on a cutting off of every intention to understand and on an avoidance of every questioning about the ground? Can such an obviousness pass as a substitute for a foundation? No. For what is obvious in the genuine sense is only what by itself precludes further inquiry as impossible, in such a way that thereby clarity reigns concerning the intelligibility of the obviousness.

§13. *The foundation of the traditional conception of truth in the return to its origin.*

Only one way still remains for us to arrive at a foundation of the traditional conception of truth as correctness. We will investigate the origin of this tradition and examine how this determination of truth was grounded when it was first established, namely in the philosophy of Aristotle. If we turn back there, our reflection also gains the advantage of being able to bring to the inner eyes, in its primordial originality and purity, the conception of truth that has been valid ever since. Hence we are suddenly confronted with the task of a historiographical consideration of the theory of truth and judgment in Aristotle, whose philosophy stems from the fourth century before Christ.

Now, if we view this historiographical task in the larger and proper perspective of our question, we will become disconcerted. For the decisive intention of our questioning is precisely to free us from the past—not because it is past, but because it is groundless. We want to raise questions on the basis of our own present and future necessities. Instead of that, we are now preparing to lose ourselves in a historiographical consideration of the past. That must signify a renunciation and a flight in the face of what is needed, namely to ask questions ourselves instead of merely reporting the opinions of bygone ages. It seems that such a historiographical consideration acts against our own intention. Therefore we need a clarification of the foundational issues—especially with reference to the further course of our lectures.

a) The historiographical consideration of the past.

Entering into history is perhaps not always and necessarily such a flight in face of the tasks of the present. It is certainly possible to consider the past from the viewpoints and according to the standards of the living present. In doing so, the past is loosened from its frozen state and is related to the present and made contemporary. Such a consideration of the past becomes a veritable reconnaissance of it; for that is the very meaning of the word historiography [*Historie*]: ἱστορεῖν—to explore. To us, therefore, historiography means an exploration of the past from the perspective of the present. This perspective can thereby become self-evident and standard. For example, Ranke, in conscious opposition to the presumed historical constructions of Hegel, believes he is presenting the past just as it was, yet definite guidelines of interpretation are directing him too—it is just that these are other than the Hegelian. Conversely, the standards may be taken from the present and applied expressly as such, and then the past is explicitly made contemporary. These two sorts of historiographical consideration are not basically distinct.

To be sure, a question remains: if the standards and guidelines of a historiographical consideration are taken—expressly or not—from what is then the present, is it thereby already decided that these standards are sufficient to grasp the past? The fact that a present is present, and what is current is today, does not guarantee that the present standards correspond to what may be the greatness of a past and are commensurable with it. Indeed, every past can be presented as timely for any age. This is the source of the confusion of all historiographical considerations. But it could also be that a present is as frozen as the past, and that the standards of a present are merely bad residues of a past no longer understood. It could be that a present is altogether caught up in itself and therefore precisely closed and shut off against what the past has to say. The mere relating of the past to what is currently present can attain new results, and even does so necessarily, for a present is always different than the previous one. But these new historiographical results, which intoxicate people and make them think themselves superior in relation to earlier historiographical science, are also already antiquated before they become truly new, because the present soon again turns into an other, and timeliness is most inconstant. Therefore all historiographical considerations are snares.

b) Historical reflection on the future, the future as the beginning of all happenings.

But a historiographical consideration does not exhaust the possible relation to history; so far from doing so, it actually impedes such a relation and cuts it off. What we are calling historical reflection is essentially different from a historiographical consideration. If we consciously elaborate the distinction between the historiographical and the historical even linguistically, and adhere to it over and against the ordinary confusion of the two terms, then this precision in the use of words is founded on a basic attitude of thought. The word "historical" [*geschichtlich*] means "happening" [*das Geschehen*], history itself as a being. "Historiographical" refers to a kind of cognition. We will not speak of historical "consideration" but "reflection." For reflection [*Be-sinnung*] is looking for the meaning [*Sinn*] of a happening, the meaning of history. "Meaning" refers here to the open region of goals, standards, impulses, decisive possibilities, and powers—all these belong *essentially* to happening.

Happening as a way to *be* is proper only to humanity. Man *has* history because he alone can *be* historical, i.e., can stand and does stand in that open region of goals, standards, drives, and powers, by withstanding this region and existing in the mode of forming, directing, acting, carrying out, and tolerating. Only man is historical—as that being which, exposed to beings as a whole, and in commerce with these beings, sets himself free in the midst of necessity. All non-human beings are history-less, though, in a derived sense, they can be historical, and are even necessarily so, insofar as they belong within the circuit of the commerce of man with beings. For example, a work of art possesses its history as work. This implies, however, that it does so on the basis of its being created by man, or, more precisely, on the basis of its opening up, as work, and keeping open, the world of man.

It is now clear that happenings and history are not what is bygone and what is considered as such, i.e., the historiographical. But just as little is this happening the present. The happening and the happenings of history are primordially and always the future, that which in a concealed way comes toward us, a revelatory process that puts us at risk, and thus is compelling in advance. The future is the beginning of all happening. Everything is enclosed within the beginning. Even if what has already begun and what has already become seem forthwith to have gone beyond their beginning, yet the latter—apparently having become the past—remains in power and abides, and everything futural encounters it. In all genuine history, which is more than a mere sequence of events, the future is decisive: i.e., what is decisive are the goals of creative activity, their rank, and their extent. The greatness of creative activity takes its measure from the extent of its power to follow up the innermost hidden law of the beginning and to carry the course of this law to its end. Therefore the new, the deviating, and the elapsed are historically unessential though nonetheless inevitable. But because the beginning is always the most concealed, because it is inexhaustible and withdraws, and because on the other hand what has already been becomes immediately the habitual, and because this conceals the beginning through its extension, therefore what has become habitual needs transformations, i.e., revolutions. Thus the original and genuine relation to the beginning is the revolutionary, which, through the upheaval of the habitual, once again liberates the hidden law of the beginning. Hence the conservative does not preserve the beginning—it does not even reach the beginning. For the conservative attitude transforms what has already become into the regular and the ideal, which is then sought ever anew in historiographical considerations.

RECAPITULATION

1) The ambiguity of the question of truth. The essence is not what is indifferently universal but what is most essential.

The question of truth is ambiguous. "We seek the truth:" that means we want to know the *true* upon which our acting and "Being" are posited. "We are asking the question of truth": that means we are endeavoring to find the *essence* of what is true. Essence is understood here as that which makes whatever is true true. When we aim at the essence, individual truths do not matter. Therefore the question of truth, in the sense of the question of its essence, immediately encounters the deepest suspicion; for we desire what is true, why should we be concerned with truth itself? To be sure, it is presupposed here without further reflection that the essence is a universal which applies to every particular instance in the same way—indifferently. But this might be to misunderstand the essence. Therefore our reflection must reach the point, indeed as soon as possible, where the question of what the essence itself is becomes unavoidable. It might turn out that the essence of something is not the indifferent but what is most essential. In that case we would have to reverse the apparently obvious demand—"We desire what is true, why should we be concerned with truth itself?"—and say instead: "We desire truth, why should we be concerned with the true?" For then precisely truth, the essence of the true, would be what is genuinely true, that which is desired in the just-mentioned demand, though sought on a by-way.

2) The problematic character of the obviousness of the traditional conception of truth, and the question of its legitimacy.

The first steps of our deliberations have already shown that we are not striving for an indifferent definition of the essence of the true, in order to be appeased by it. We freed ourselves from the customary determination of truth as the correctness of an assertion by showing how this determination is based on a more original one that constitutes the ground of the possibility of correctness.

But as unavoidably as we were led to acknowledge an openness—as we called it—that is precisely how dubious it has become whether we have indeed liberated ourselves from the customary conception of truth through this return to openness as the ground of correctness. In fact we are relying precisely on the customary conception, so much so that we are seeking a foundation for this reliance and consequently want to confirm it all the more.

We rely on the customary conception of truth as correctness, without having founded this conception sufficiently. We come by it as something traditional. The appeal to what has been handed down, the so-called "tradition," is not a foundation. Not even if the traditional has become obvious. Obviousness is always a very problematic assurance of the legitimacy of an intuition. For, on the one hand, it is questionable to what extent that which is supposed to be obvious to the understanding is really understood or whether we have here precisely a renunciation of the will to understand and the appeal to thoughtlessness elevated to a principle. On the other hand, it could be asked what kind of intelligibility or understanding is providing the standard here. What might be very obvious on a certain level of understanding—the most superficial—can be wholly unintelligible on the plane of the will to genuine comprehension.

If, consequently, the customary determination of truth as correctness appears to us correct precisely when we reflect no further on it, then this "obviousness" is not yet a sufficient foundation for the delimitation of the essence of the true.

3) Toward the foundation of the customary conception of truth through a historical reflection on its origin. The distinction between a historiographical consideration and a historical reflection.

Therefore, in order to gain the foundation of the customary conception of truth, we will question back and examine how it was founded when it was first put forth. Thus we are forced to turn to the philosophy of Aristotle. That means that instead of actually asking the question of truth by ourselves and for ourselves, i.e., for the future, we will lose ourselves in historiographical considerations and reports about the ancient past.

What is happening here? Are we really acting contrary to our own intentions by returning to history? No. But we can only understand that a reflection on history belongs precisely and essentially to the will to shape the future if we distinguish between a historiographical consideration and a historical reflection.

The historiographical, as the word itself is supposed to indicate, refers to the past insofar as it is explored and presented, either expressly or inexpressly, from the perspective of what happens to be the present. Every historiographical consideration turns the past as such into an object. Even where a "historiography" of the present is put forth, the very present must already be bygone. All historiography is retrospective, even when it makes the past timely.

The historical does not denote a manner of grasping and exploring but the very happening itself. The historical is not the past, not even the present, but the future, that which is commended to the will, to expectation, to care. This does not allow itself to be "considered"; instead, we must "reflect" on it. We have to be concerned with the meaning, the possible standards, the necessary goals, the ineluctable powers, and that from which all human happenings begin. These goals and powers can be such that they have already come to pass—in a hidden way—long ago but are precisely therefore not the past but what still abides and is awaiting the liberation of its influence. The future is the origin of history. What is most futural, however, is the great beginning, that which—withdrawing itself constantly—reaches back the farthest and at the same time reaches forward the farthest. The hidden destiny of all beginnings, however, is to seem to be thrust aside, overcome, and refuted by what they themselves begin and by what follows them. The ordinary character of what is henceforth the ordinary becomes the lord over what is for ever the extraordinary character of the beginning. Therefore, in order to rescue the beginning, and consequently the future as well, from time to time the domination of the ordinary and all too ordinary must be broken. An upheaval is needed, in order that the extraordinary and the forward-reaching might be liberated and come to power. Revolution, the upheaval of what is habitual, is the genuine relation to the beginning. The conservative, on the contrary, the preserving, adheres to and retains only what was begun in the wake of the beginning and what has come forth from it. The beginning can never be grasped through mere preservation, because to begin means to think and to act from the perspective of the future and of what is extraordinary, and from the renunciation of the crutches and evasions of the habitual and the usual.

To be sure, even the conservative, the adherence to what has become, and the mere preservation and care for the hitherto, needs, as a human attitude, standards and guidelines. But it draws them from what has become and sees therein the regular or the rule, and elevates this to an ideal—which is then retrieved everywhere and required again, and through this "ever again" gains an apparently supratemporal validity.

c) The acquisition of the beginning in the experience of its law. The historical as the extension from the future into the past and from the past into the future.

What is conservative remains bogged down in the historiographical; only what is revolutionary attains the depth of history. Revolution does not mean here mere subversion and destruction but an upheaval and recreating of the customary so that the beginning might be restructured. And because the original belongs to the beginning, the restructuring of the beginning is never the poor imitation of what was earlier; it is entirely other and nevertheless the same.

The beginning never allows itself to be represented or considered in historiography. For, in that way, i.e., historiographically considered, it is degraded into something which has already become and is no longer beginning. The beginning is only acquired when we creatively experience its law, and this law can never become a rule but remains specific and particular, the uniqueness of the necessary. The uniqueness of the necessary is that simple which, as the most difficult, must ever and again be accomplished completely anew.

Historiographical considerations attain only the past and never reach the historical. For the latter goes beyond everything historiographical, just as much in the direction of the future as with respect to the past, and all the more in relation to the present.

The present, with the inevitable obtrusiveness of its results, certainly appears to offer in the most immediate way that which comes to pass, and yet history is precisely in any present what comes to pass most genuinely and is thus the most hidden. Therefore a historiographical consideration and presentation of the present is the most blind over and against history. This kind of historiography touches only the foremost of the foreground, which is, of course, taken by the common understanding as what genuinely comes to pass.

The historical is the super-historiographical but for that reason is precisely not the supra-temporal, not the so-called eternal or timeless, since the historiographical only reaches the past and not the genuinely temporal. The properly temporal is the stirring, exciting, but at the same time conserving and preserving extension and stretch from the future into the past and from the latter into the former. In this extension, man as historical is in each case a "spread." The present is always later than the future; it is the last. It springs from the struggle of the future with the past. That the coming to pass of history emerges out of the future does not mean, however, that history can be made and directed by planning. Rather, man—precisely in creative shaping—can penetrate into the uncertain and incalculable only by means of the *will* to provide a direction within what is necessary and out of a knowledge of the law of the beginning.

Historical reflections are fundamentally different from historiographical considerations. Historiography has, however, its own proper usefulness as instruction, mediation of cognitions, and as research and presentation; and accordingly it also has its own limits. Historical reflection, on the contrary, is possible, and indeed necessary, only where history is grasped creatively and co-formatively—in the creation of the poet, the architect, the thinker, the statesman. These are never historiographers when they reflect on what comes to pass. Since they are not historiographers, they accomplish the opening up and the new foundation of history. Historical reflection is never the exploration of the past, even if this past presents the spirit of an age. All "history of the spirit" is always only historiography but easily creates the impression of being a reflection, since it does investigate the spirit. But there the spirit is only an object—set aside and represented as something that once was and is now past and perhaps is still romantically longed for. On the other hand, Jakob Burckhardt, who at times seems to be an "inexact" historiographer or a pedant with literary ambitions, is anything but a historiographer. He is a thinker of history through and through, to whom historiographical science and philology only provide auxiliary services.

So much for a first, though not yet decisive, clarification of the distinction between a historiographical consideration and a historical reflection.

§14. *Return to the Aristotelian doctrine of the truth of the assertion as a historical reflection.*

If now, in the context of an original posing of the basic question of truth, we refer back to Aristotle in order to reflect on the foundation of the traditional concept of truth following the guideline of his theory of the truth of the assertion, then this has nothing to do with a historiographical consideration of a past doctrine of an allegedly antiquated Greek philosophy. This is so not only because the problematic Aristotelian conception of truth is not bygone, and still today thoroughly determines our knowledge and decisions, but also because we are questioning the inauguration and preservation of the ordinary Western concept of truth at its very outset and are doing so only in terms of our awakening the question of truth for the future as a—or perhaps *the*—basic question of philosophy. This questioning—should it succeed—will itself stand within a history whose beginning reaches back temporally behind Aristotle and whose future reaches far beyond us. Therefore, the philosophical thought of the Greeks that we are reflecting on is not something bygone, nor is it something of today, made to fit the times. It is futural and therefore super-historiographical; it is the historical.

The essence of truth is not a mere concept, carried about in the head. On the contrary, truth is alive; in the momentary form of its essence it is the power that determines everything true and untrue; it is what is sought after, what is fought for, what is suffered for. The essence of truth is a happening, more real and more efficacious than all historiographical occurrences and facts, because it is their ground. What is historical in all history comes to pass in that great silence for which man only rarely has the right ear. That we know so little or even nothing of this hidden history of the essence of truth is no proof of its unreality but only evidence of our lack of reflective power. If we now distinguish, in our representations, between a historiographical consideration and a historical reflection, nothing is gained as long as we do not carry out that distinction and put it to the test in a real historical reflection. Yet we had to providc this first reference to the distinction, at least in order to obviate a misinterpretation of what follows as a mere report about doctrines long bygone.

§15. *The Aristotelian foundation of the correctness of an assertion as the essence of truth.*

Because our discussion of Greek philosophy is not a historiographical addendum but belongs to the very course of our questioning, this course must be constantly surveyed and dominated. Let us therefore briefly repeat the task. Through a first reflection, the traditional conception of truth as correctness became questionable. Something worthy of questioning showed itself: that multiple-unitary openness of beings, on the basis of which a conformity to something in representation, and consequently correctness, first become possible. If we conceive and understand this openness as the ground of the possibility of correctness, we touch upon truth in its original and proper essence. But the return to this openness leads to the original essence of truth only if it can be shown in advance with good foundation that correctness already in some way contains, even if not originally, the essence of truth. What is the case here? Is the interpretation of truth as the correctness of a representation or assertion a founded one, and how so? In order to gain some clarity, we will ask this question in view of the primordial positing of the definition of truth in Aristotle. The return to the Aristotelian doctrine is not to be a mere historiographical consideration but a historical reflection.

The first step would be to recount Aristotle's doctrine of the essence of the true and the false, and then discuss the appurtenance of truth and falsity to the assertion (λόγος) and the structure of the assertion itself. But because the contemporary theory of truth and of the assertion is not essentially distinct from Aristotle's and has already been more or less elucidated with the example of the proposition, "The stone is hard," we may here forego an elaborate presentation of Aristotle's doctrine.

Instead, we will ask immediately: how does Aristotle ground this determination of the essence of truth? With what legitimacy is the essence of truth determined to be the correctness of an assertion? The foundation for this essential determination appears to be easy, since it is obvious. It can be shown that in an assertion of the type, "The stone is hard," there occurs a conformity of the representation to the object. But is that appeal to the *occurrence* of correctness in this or in another proposition a foundation for the *essence* of truth as correctness? By no means. Such references to correct propositions only provide examples of correctness but not the legitimating foundation for the essence and for an essential determination. The question is not whether and how the essence of truth could be elucidated through the example of a correct proposition, but whether and how the positing of the correctness of the assertion as the essence of truth is founded. This includes the question of how the essence of something is to be posited at all and where this positing of the essence would have its principle and ground. Obviously, this question can be answered only if we have first clarified what essence is as such, whether it be the essence of truth or the essence of a plant or the essence of a work of art.

§16. *The turning of the question of the essence of truth into the question of the truth (essentiality) of the essence. The question of the Aristotelian conception of the essentiality of the essence.*

What makes up the essence of the essence or, as we say, essentiality? Essentiality indicates what the essence as such really is, what it is in truth. It delimits the truth of the essence. We look in vain for the foundation of an essential determination—in our case, the determination of the essence of truth—if we do not truly know what in general is to be determined here and is to be founded in its determination, namely the essence itself.

Where have we arrived? Perhaps we now have some inkling of the remarkable character of the way forced upon us by the question of truth itself, if we relentlessly enough raise questions in order to create a free path for its innermost impetus. We are asking the question of truth, i.e., we are asking about the essence of truth. We are not seeking individual "truths" but the essence of truth. In the unfolding of this question we have now reached the point of having to raise the question of the truth of essence. All this is enigmatic: the question of the essence of truth is at the same time and in itself the question of the truth of the essence. The question of truth—asked as a basic question—turns itself in itself against itself. This turning, which we have now run up against, is an intimation of the fact that we are entering the compass of a genuine philosophical question. We cannot now say what the turning means, where it is founded, since we have hardly entered the portico of the region of philosophical reflection. Only one thing is clear: if all philosophical thought must more unavoidably move in this turning the more it thinks originally, i.e., the more it approaches what in philosophy is primordially and always thought and reflected upon, then the turning must belong essentially to the single focus of philosophical reflection (Being as the appropriating event).

Since it was necessary to bring a first clarity to the task of the question of truth, the search for what is true, whether it be individual truths or the decisive truth, was delimited against a reflection on the *essence* of truth. This delimitation seemed unequivocal, and the philosophical task thereby seemed clear. Now, however, we have seen that in the question of the essence of truth not only is truth as such questionable but so is the perspective within which we are raising the question: what we so casually and easily call the essence. We speak of the essence of the state, the essence of life, the essence of technology, conceding perhaps that we do not yet know the essence of the state, of life, and of technology, though silently claiming to know the other side, namely what essence is in general, whether it be a matter of the state, life, technology, etc. But as obvious, and questionable, as is the determination of truth as correctness, that is how questionable, and obvious, is our view of the essentiality of the essence, supposing that in the usual talk about the essence of things we do intend something determinate in the word "essence" and do not simply abandon ourselves to an undetermined word-sound.

Therefore in order to decide how Aristotle laid the foundation for the subsequent common interpretation of the essence of truth, we have to know how he conceived the essence as such, the essentiality of the essence, especially since the Aristotelian determination of the essentiality of the essence became the standard one for the times that followed and remains valid, despite some modifications, even today. But we must again renounce a detailed presentation of the Aristotelian doctrine of the essentiality of the essence. For to do it satisfactorily, a far-reaching interpretation, especially of the seventh book of the *Metaphysics*, would have to be articulated. Within the context of our lectures what matters is only the basic thrust of the Aristotelian determination of the essentiality of the essence, i.e., that which corresponds to, and springs forth as, the inner law of the beginning of Occidental thinking, and which received from Plato its decisive stamp for all subsequent Western thought.

RECAPITULATION

1) Rejection of three misinterpretations of the distinction between historiographical consideration and historical reflection. Science and historical reflection.

The present discussions in the history of philosophy, as well as those to come later in the lecture course, are to be understood in the light of the distinction between a historiographical consideration and a historical reflection. Admittedly, the distinction and what is distinguished in it have not been examined here thoroughly in every respect. Therefore the possibility of misunderstanding will inevitably persist. Yet three conspicuous misinterpretations should expressly be rejected:

1. Since we said historical reflection is accomplished only by creative thinkers within various domains, one might suppose that it can treat the past with completely unbounded freedom. But historical reflection is in fact bound to the past in an essentially more rigorous way than historiography is. For what historical reflection remembers in the past is one and the same as the future, which the creators establish, and grasp as law, in their de-

cisions concerning their tasks. Contrary to this, the points of view of historiography toward the past are very arbitrary, and insofar as historiography as a science is concerned, they are chosen and evaluated primarily according to whether, and how far, they promote new historiographical cognitions, i.e., insofar as they enhance the progress of the science. Although contemporary historiography has accommodated itself to an insistent timeliness of viewpoints, yet, according to the still unbroken idea of science, every historiographical constatation is important and relevant as a building stone for historiographical overviews (syntheses). Historiography is bound by past facts, interpreted in a certain way each time; historical reflection, however, is bound by that happening on the basis of which facts can arise and can be in the first place. Historical reflection is subject to a higher and more rigorous law than historiography is, although it might seem, judging by appearances, that the reverse obtains.

2. Since historiographical considerations are always subordinated to historical reflections, the erroneous opinion can arise to the effect that historiography is altogether superfluous for history. But from the order of rank just mentioned the only conclusion to be drawn is this: historiographical considerations are essential only insofar as they are supported by a historical reflection, are directed by it in their very way of questioning, and are determined by it in the delimitation of their tasks. But this also implies the converse, that historiographical considerations and cognitions are indeed indispensable. And that holds all the more for an age which has to set itself free from the trammels of historiography and its confusion with history. This liberation is necessary because a creative era has to protect itself equally against an often ignorant and weak imitation of the past, and against an irreverent submerging of the past—two attitudes, apparently mutually opposed, which all too readily find themselves unified, though in itself this unity is thoroughly confused.

3. Finally, one might think that this distinction between historiographical consideration and historical reflection is empty conceptual hair-splitting, unnecessary and a dead letter. Let us show this is not the case through a peculiar and apparently extraneous example.

It is a well-known fact that the natural sciences admit a historiographical consideration of their own past merely as an addendum, since for them what is past is simply what is no longer. Natural science itself only deals with present nature. This attitude was expressed some time ago by a famous mathematician during a debate over the occupancy of a professorial chair in classical philology. He declared that this chair should be replaced by one in physical science, and his argument was the following: classical philology always deals only with what has already been; the natural sciences, on the contrary, consider not only what is presently real, but they can also predict, and can calculate in advance how the real has to be, and in that way can lay the foundations of technology. Thus, the historiography of natural science merely consists in past discoveries and theories, ones that have been overcome long ago through progress. The "history" of science is for science itself its historiography, that which the science constantly leaves behind in its progress to ever new results. The historiography of natural science does not belong to it or to its methodology. Through historiographical considerations of the sequence of earlier theories and discoveries one can at most clarify how magnificently far we have come and how backward earlier times had been, dominated by "philosophy" and "speculation" with their unbridled dreams, which have now finally been shattered by the exact and sober consideration of the "facts." In this way historiography can establish that a philosopher, such as Aristotle, was of the opinion that heavy bodies fall faster than light ones, whereas the "facts" of modern science prove that all bodies fall equally fast. A historiographical consideration of such a kind is therefore an account of a growth in progress, whereby whatever happens to be new is interpreted as more progressive.

But above and beyond historiography, we still claim that historical reflection is possible and will even one day prove to be indispensable. Historical reflection will question the basic experience and basic conception of the Greeks, or of Aristotle in particular, about "nature," the body, motion, place, and time. And historical reflection will recognize that the Greek and the Aristotelian basic experience of nature was of such a kind that the velocity of the fall of heavy and light bodies and their belonging to a certain place could not have been seen otherwise or determined differently than they were. A historical reflection will realize that the Greek theory of natural processes did not rest on insufficient observation but on an other—perhaps even deeper—conception of nature that precedes all particular observations. For Aristotle, "physics" means precisely the metaphysics of nature.

A historical reflection will discern that even the modern science of nature is grounded on a metaphysics—in such an unconditional way and so firmly and so much a matter of course that most scientists do not suspect it in the least. A historical reflection on the foundations of modern natural science will perceive that the much-acclaimed facts, which modern experimental science accepts as the sole reality, become visible as facts and can be founded only in light of a wholly determined metaphysics of nature, a metaphysics that is not less operative because contemporary scientists are no longer acquainted with it. On the other hand, the great scientists who laid the foundations of modern natural science were great precisely in that they possessed the power and the passion of foundational thinking and had the education for it as well.

A historical reflection will acknowledge that it makes utterly no sense to measure the Aristotelian theory of motion straightforwardly against the results of the research of Galileo and to judge the former as antiquated, the latter as progressive; for in these two cases nature means something entirely different. According to historiographical calculation, modern natural science is certainly more advanced than the Greek, assuming the technological domination, and thereby also the destruction, of nature is indeed progress—versus the preservation of nature as a metaphysical power. From the standpoint of historical reflection, the advanced modern science of nature is not a whit more true than the Greek; on the contrary, at most it is more untrue, because it is altogether caught in the web of its own methodology, and, notwithstanding all its discoveries, it lets escape what is genuinely the object of these discoveries: namely nature, and man's relation to it, and man's place in it.

The historiographical comparison and account of the past and the present conclude in the progressiveness of the present. Historical reflection on the past and on the future leads to an insight into the groundlessness of the contemporary relation (or lack of relation) to nature; it leads to the insight that the natural sciences, as in general all sciences, in spite of their progress, or perhaps precisely because of this progress, find themselves in a crisis. Indeed, as we hear today, "The prattle about the crisis of science should finally be toned down" (immatriculation discourse of the present rector, December, 1937). The "crisis" of science does certainly *not* consist in its not allowing professorships in paleontology, ethnology, ethnography, etc., nor does it consist in its not being relevant enough to life—that it is all too much. We would do well to stop speaking of the crisis of science in such terms. For these decriers of the crisis are in fact basically in complete accord with contemporary science, embrace it, and even become its best defenders, as soon as they find a satisfying position within it. The crisis is quite otherwise and stems not from 1933, and not from 1918, and not even from the much-criticized nineteenth century, but from the beginning of the modern age, which was not a mistake but a fate, and only a fate will overcome it.

The most acute crisis of today's science might consist precisely in having no suspicion of the crisis in which it is involved: in other words, in believing that it has been sufficiently confirmed by its successes and its palpable results. But nothing spiritual, and nothing which is to dominate as a spiritual power and is supposed to be more than a business, can ever be validated by success and usefulness.

Historical reflections question the present and future of science itself and heap shame on its belief in progress, for such reflections show that in matters of essence there is no progress but only the transformation of the same. For natural science, and for any science, historiographical considerations are perhaps only an extrinsic concession to let its own past be seen as something to overcome. Historical reflection, on the contrary, belongs to the essence of all the sciences, insofar as it claims to prepare and to form for them, beyond every useful result, an essential knowledge of their subject matter and of the concomitant region of Being.

The sciences and certainly, in the ultimate analysis, their establishment today in their total administrative organization (the university) are far from suspecting anything of the necessity of historical reflection. Why? Because this presumably only abstract distinction between historiographical consideration and historical reflection is neither experienced nor grasped and for the time being will not be grasped. For we have long ago become used to the fact that a scientist can refer to acknowledged accomplishments in his field and at the same time, with a disturbing unsuspecting innocence, may be blind to all that provides his science foundation and legitimacy. We even think this to be wondrous. We have long ago fallen into the most silly Americanism, whose principle is that the true is what succeeds and everything else is "speculation," i.e., a dream far removed from life. We wallow again already—all those who a short time ago were still facing each other as hostile brothers but always belonged fundamentally together—in a jovial and even tipsy optimism which lets come to life again the *Gaudeamus igitur* and the *Ergo bibamus* as the coronation of academic life (immatriculation discourse of the dean of the school of medicine). How often and for how long must we Germans again and again be struck with blindness?

Optimism is a beautiful thing; but it is only the repression of pessimism, and both pessimism and its counterpart arise only on the basis of a conception of reality, and consequently of history, in the sense of a business, the prospects of which now are calculated as hopeful and now as the opposite. Optimism and pessimism exist only within the compass of a historiographical consideration of history. Optimists are not people who get rid of pessimism—for what other reason would they have to be optimists? Historical reflection, on the other hand, stands outside of this opposition between optimism and pessimism, since it does not count on the bliss of progress and still less on an unfortunate arrest of progress or even regress. Instead, historical reflection works toward the preparation of a historical existence which lives up to the *greatness* of fate, to the peak moments of Being.

These remarks have been intended to indicate that the distinction between historiographical consideration and historical reflection is not a free-floating "speculative" construction of thought but represents the most stern necessity of a decision whose acceptance or neglect is decisive for ourselves and for our destiny in history (and also for the German university, in which we are looking ahead, according to the opinion of the many, who are thoughtless by profession, to the most marvelous times as in the days of Wilhelm II).

2) The path from the question of the essence of truth to the question of the truth (essentiality) of the essence.

The task of these lectures compels us to historical reflection. We are raising the question of truth. We entered into the ordinary and long-standing traditional conception of truth as the correctness of an assertion. We found in this conception something worthy of questioning—that openness of beings over and against man and of man for beings. We appealed to this openness as the ground of the possibility of correctness. The ground is the more original. Therefore the question-worthy openness must comprise the more original essence of truth. To be sure, this is so only under the presupposition that the traditional conception of truth for its part expresses already in general something of the essence of truth and does so with good foundation. What is the case here?

How and through what was this conception of the essence of truth as the correctness of an assertion founded when Aristotle introduced it? How can a claim about the essence be founded in the first place, whether it be the essence of the true, the essence of the beautiful, the essence of plants, the essence of technology, etc.? Just how are we to understand the essence of something? What, in truth, do we mean by the word "essence"? In short, where does the truth of the essence lie?

While we were asking about the essence of truth and wanted to lay the foundation for a determination of the essence of truth, we were driven to the question of the truth of the essence. That is quite in order, insofar as a philosophical question is at stake. Because in such questioning nothing may remain unquestioned. If we ask about the essence of truth, and make no attempt to clarify our understanding of what is meant by essence, then we are only half asking; from a philosophical standpoint, we are not questioning at all.

Since we are now questioning how Aristotle founded the determination of the essence of the true, we must clarify what he understood by "essence." That is the more necessary since the characterization of the essentiality and the truth of the essence in Aristotle and Plato became for posterity, right up to the present moment, the standard one, as did their determination of the essence of truth. And this connection is not accidental.

Chapter Two

The Question of the Truth (Essentiality) of the Essence

§17. *Historical reflection on the Aristotelian-Platonic determination of the essentiality of the essence.*

a) The four characteristics of the essentiality of the essence in Aristotle.

We will now attempt to reflect on the Aristotelian-Platonic determination of the essentiality of the essence. The "essence" of a thing, so it is said, is one and universal and applies to the many particular instances. The essence "table" indicates what applies, as something one and the same, to every table as table. The universal is therefore a standard "over" the whole extent of its real and possible particularizations. The Greeks use the word κατά (cf. κατηγορία) to signify what extends over particulars and holds for them from "above." The whole which includes every particular within itself is called ὅλον. Accordingly, the essence is what holds for many: τὸ καθόλου.

This essence, as it were, hovers over the particular and is therefore also conceived as γένος. We usually translate this as "genus" or "class": table in general is the class with regard to the species: dinner table, writing table, sewing table, which "really" occur themselves first in their repeatedly varied particularizations. Γένος, however, in the more original sense of the word, means lineage, derivation, origin. Only by the prevailing domination of logic did γένος as origin become γένος as class in the sense of the higher universality of the "type."

The essence is that from which a particular thing, and indeed in *what* it is, has its origin, whence it derives. Therefore the essence of a thing, of any particular whatever, can be conceived as that which the thing already in a certain sense "was" before it became the singular thing it "is." For if there were not already—no matter how—something like table in general, then never could any particular table be fabricated; what the particular table is supposed to be as a table would be altogether lacking. Therefore Aristotle also conceived the essence as the Being (εἶναι) of the particular being, what it—the particular—already was (τί ἦν) before it became this particular. The essence was thus expressed accordingly: τὸ τί ἦν εἶναι.

All these determinations of the essentiality of the essence, τὸ καθόλου (the general), τὸ γένος (the origin), τὸ τί ἦν εἶναι (the Being it was) conceive the essence as that which lies in advance of particular things and so lies at their foundation—ὑπο/κείμενον.

We are now in a position to understand the statement by which Aristotle begins his own proper examination of the essence as such: λέγεται δ' ἡ οὐσία, εἰ μὴ πλεοναχῶς, ἀλλ' ἐν τέτταρσί γε μάλιστα:[1] "The 'essence' {preliminary translation following the usual interpretation} is named (and represented) predominately in four ways, if not still more manifoldly." καὶ γὰρ τὸ τί ἦν εἶναι καὶ τὸ καθόλου καὶ τὸ γένος οὐσία δοκεῖ εἶναι ἑκάστου, καὶ τέταρτον τούτων τὸ ὑποκείμενον:[2] "For the 'Being it was' and also the general and likewise the origin seem to form the essence of particular things, and similarly the fourth of the characterizations: the underlying foundation."

That Aristotle speaks here about δοκεῖ ("it seems so") indicates that he himself will not allow these four characterizations of the essence predelineated by Platonic philosophy as determinations of essentiality. How Aristotle specifically decides (eliminating καθόλου and γένος) will be shown in our discussion of that part of his treatise (*Met.* Z).

1. Aristotle, *Metaphysica*. Ed. W. Christ, Leipzig 1886. Z 3, 1028b 33ff.
2. Ibid.

b) The essence as the whatness of a being. Whatness as ἰδέα: the constantly present, what is in view in advance, the look (εἶδος).

We are reflecting only on what is fundamental in the determination of the essentiality of the essence, as it was stated once and for all in the Platonic-Aristotelian philosophy and became normative for posterity. That is, we are reflecting on what we ourselves ordinarily mean—even if in a very indeterminate way—when we speak about the "essence" of a thing. Insofar as we are successful in determining more precisely what we mean by essence we will also be capable of examining more exactly how the essence of something—e.g., the essence of truth—is posited, grasped, and founded, and what sort of foundation belongs to truth itself, according to its essence.

The first characterization Aristotle brings up with regard to the essence is that it contains the universal—e.g., the essence table is that which is common to all individual tables and therefore in an assertion about them is valid for all tables. Plato had already characterized the essence as what is common over and against the particularizations and had designated it with the name τὸ κοινόν. Ever since then, this characterization of the essence as the universal has remained the most usual one. But it is also in fact the most superficial, for no extended deliberation is needed to see that the characterization of the essence as κοινόν, as what is common to many, is not sufficient. The essence of the table is not the essence *because* it is valid for many particular tables, real or possible, but the reverse: only insofar as it is the essence can it apply to the individual tables. The character of the κοινόν cannot be the genuinely distinctive mark of the essence but is only a possible consequence of the essence. We must say "possible," because if we ask about the essence of Plato or of Frederick the Great, then we are certainly seeking the essence of these individual men, but here it is the essence of something which is, by its very "nature," precisely singular and unique—a kind of essence that precisely excludes being valid for many.

In this way it is clear that what is essential in the essence cannot be the κοινόν but that which admits, or demands, that the essence be valid for the many individuals. But what is that? What do these two thinkers say who have decisively determined all Western speech and thought about the essence of things?

Reviewing the rest of Aristotle's characterizations of the essence, we come upon a determination that is so simple it says nothing to us: the essence is what we seek when we ask τί ἐστιν: *what* is this? What is this here and that there? A plant, a house. The essence is the τί εἶναι—the whatness [*Wassein*] of a being. To ask *what* something is is all too familiar to us and to earlier generations. What something is is its essence. But what is this "what" itself? Is there an answer? To be sure. Plato provided it. What something is, the whatness (τὸ τί εἶναι), e.g., of a house or a man, is what is constantly present in that something. In all ever so different houses what is constant is *what* they are, "house," and conversely, *what* they *are*, houses in all their variety and change, is the constant. A house could not collapse if it were not a house.

This constant presence is what we have in view in advance, though without considering it explicitly, when we name and experience whatever we encounter as what it is, e.g., as a house. When we enter a house we pay attention to the door, the staircase, the halls, and the rooms, and only to these, for otherwise we could not move around in it at all. On the other hand, we do not pay attention explicitly and in the same way to what all that is in its unity, namely house. Nevertheless, precisely what it is, house, the essence, is always sighted in advance, though not explicitly considered. In fact, if we did engage in such a consideration of the essence we would never come to enter the house and live in it. Nevertheless, again, what the thing is, the constantly present, must be sighted in advance and indeed necessarily so. "To see" is in Greek ἰδεῖν; what is in sight, precisely as sighted, is ἰδέα. What is sighted is what the being is in advance and constantly. The "what it is," the whatness, is the ἰδέα; and conversely, the "idea" is the whatness, and the latter is the essence. More precisely, and more in the Greek vein, the ἰδέα is the *look* something offers, the aspect it has and, as it were, shows of itself, the εἶδος. Only in light of what is seen in advance and constantly, yet not explicitly observed, e.g., house, can we experience and use this door as a door, this staircase as a staircase to this storey with these rooms. If that were not in sight, how would matters then stand? You may think that out for yourselves.

"Essence"

τὸ καθόλου
τὸ γένος
τὸ τί ἦν εἶναι (*a priori*)
τὸ ὑποκείμενον (*subjectum*)
τὸ κοινόν
τὸ τί ἐστιν (*quidditas*)
τὸ εἶδος
ἰδέα
οὐσία (*essentia*)

RECAPITULATION

1) Four characterizations of the essentiality of the essence in Aristotle. The whatness in Plato: the ἰδέα as what is sighted in advance, the look.

We are abiding with the question: how does Aristotle—i.e., Greek philosophy in general—found the essence of truth and the definition of the essence of truth as the correctness of an assertion? To gain the answer we must ask immediately and before all else: how do the Greeks conceive what we call essence? In what consists for them the essentiality of the essence?

First of all with reference to Aristotle, *Metaphysics* Z, we tried to elucidate, in a few broad strokes, that and how there can still be decided something about the essentiality of the essence. The result was the following: Aristotle mentions primarily four characterizations of the essentiality of the essence; these stand in a material connection and can be synthesized in one of them.

1. The essence is what something is in general, what applies over the entire extent of the particular instances: τὸ καθόλου.

2. The essence is that from which anything, in what it is as such, has its origin, whence it stems: τὸ γένος. An individual house is of the genus: house in general.

3. The essence can therefore also be designated as what something already was, before it became what it is as an individual. An individual house is not first a house as an individual thing, but what it is as this individual thing, namely "house," was already.

And that was, not because there were already other individual houses before this one, but because, in order for this or that house to become and be what it is, something like "house in general" must exist and be given. Consequently, "house" is, with regard to the constructed individual house, what already was—τὸ τί ἦν εἶναι. With this determination is connected the one that became usual in the subsequent thinking of the West and received a special stamp in Kant's philosophy: the essence as what is prior to the thing, deriving from what is earlier: the a priori.

4. In all these determinations, the essence is what lies over or before the individual, or what lies under it as its ground: τὸ ὑποκείμενον.

After this first perspective, it was then our task to sketch more precisely what we genuinely mean by "essence," especially since our concept of essence is still entirely founded on the Greek one.

The most familiar characterization of the essence, the one that is still usual today, though also the most superficial, is the first-mentioned: the essence is τὸ καθόλου, conceived by Plato as τὸ κοινόν. A moment's reflection showed, however, that the universality and its applicability to many are not themselves the essentiality of the essence but only its consequences. The universal "table in general" is not the essence *because* it applies to many particular tables, but it applies to the many and can do so only because there is in this universal, in what is common to all the particularizations, something identical, and that is where the essence resides.

What then is this identity taken in itself, abstracting from the merely subsequent applicability to the individual instances? We said the essence is what something is, τὸ τί ἐστιν (*quidditas*). And what now is this, what something is, the whatness? No further answer seems possible. Nevertheless Plato provided an answer, an answer which became henceforth perhaps the most consequential, influential, and disastrous philosophical definition in Western thinking: the essence is what something is, and we encounter what it is as that which we constantly have in sight in all our comportment to the thing. When we enter a house and live in it we constantly have "house" in sight, i.e., house-ness. If this were not seen, we could never experience and enter stairs, hall, room, attic, or cellar. But this house-ness, which stands in view, is not thereby considered and observed the way the individual window is, toward which we walk in order to close it. House-ness is not even observed incidentally. It is not observed at all; yet it is in sight, and precisely in an eminent way: it is sighted in advance. "To see" and "to sight" are in Greek ἰδεῖν, and what is in sight, in its being sighted, is ἰδέα. What is sighted is what something is, the whatness, the essence. Hence the essence of something is the ἰδέα, and conversely the "idea," what is sighted in this determinate sense, the aspect something offers in what it is, is the essence.

2) How to understand the essence sighted in advance.

If, in our immediate comportment toward individual beings, we did not have the essence already in sight, or, Platonically expressed, if we did not have the "ideas" of individual things in view in advance, then we would be blind, and would remain blind, to everything these things are as individuals, i.e., as such and such, here and now, in these or those relations. And still more: according to the way and to the extent that we regard the essence, we are also capable of experiencing and determining what is unique in the things. What is viewed in advance and how it is in view are decisive for what we factually see in the individual thing. This basic rule, which is not at all considered by ordinary thought and is too rarely noticed in spite of all the directives pointing toward it, becomes especially clear in a counter-example. What follows is a particularly impressive one.

In the course of the battle around the citadel of Verdun, in the spring of 1916, Fort Vaux was to be stormed. The commander of the division selected for the attack was preparing for it on the night of March 8–9. During the night, a dispatch from a cavalry officer arrived at the command post of the division: "Have reached Fort Vaux with three companies." The general transmitted the message that night in the form: "Fort Vaux is taken." Immediately the whole front knew: the fort is occupied by us! At dawn, hundreds of binoculars were trained on the fort. Our black-white-red banners could be seen waving over the fort; German soldiers were seen walking on the ramparts; pyramids of our rifles were seen standing there. The crown prince personally handed out to the division commander the medal Pour le mérite. But no sooner did the crown prince leave the division headquarters than a messenger brought the news that everything was in error, the fort was still in French hands—and in fact it was.

Were the black-white-red banners, the soldiers marching around, and the rifles optical illusions? No—the ones who were looking through the binoculars saw very well, and they could not see otherwise. The mistake lay not in the seeing but in what they had in view in advance, the stormed fort, on the basis of which fore-sight they then *interpreted* in such and such a way what they saw.

Everything that we see in particulars is always determined by what we have in view in advance. The mistake did not reside in the seeing but in the imprecise dispatch of the cavalry officer, or in the faulty interpretation by division headquarters. "Have reached the fort" meant only "I am standing before the ramparts of the fort" and did not mean: "I took it." This dispatch and its interpretation and circulation created that fore-sight on the fort which then became the ὑποκείμενον for the apparently "incorrect" seeing. What is essential is not what we presumably establish with exactness by means of instruments and gadgets; what is essential is the view in advance which first opens up the field for anything to be established. So it happens that we, lost as we usually are in the activities of observing and establishing, believe we "see" many things and yet do not see what really is.

§18. *The Greek determination of the essence (whatness) in the horizon of an understanding of Being as constant presence.*

a) The determination of the essence (whatness) as the "beingness" (οὐσία) of beings. The understanding of Being as constant presence is the ground for the interpretation of beingness (οὐσία) as ἰδέα.

In Platonic terms, the view in advance of the aspect something offers, the view of its εἶδος, provides the ἰδέα, that which the thing is, its essence. Herewith the essentiality of the essence is indeed characterized quite unequivocally and beyond mere whatness: the essence is the whatness of something, and this is determined as the dominant look, ἰδέα. But how does Plato come to this characterization of the essentiality of the essence? Is it obvious?

Not in the least, although we have long ago accustomed ourselves to more or less thoughtless talk about the "Ideas." For if the essence is identified with what something is, with the whatness, then the essence characterizes what a being *is* as such. In the essence as whatness or what-it-*is*, there resides therefore a conception of the being with regard to its Being. A being is in Greek τὸ ὄν, and what universally determines a being as a being is the κοινόν, the being in its beingness [*Seiendheit*], the ὄν in its οὐσία. Because the Greeks conceive the essence as the whatness of something and interpret the latter as "Idea," therefore the essence means the same as the being*ness* of beings, οὐσία, and therefore the οὐσία of the ὄν is the ἰδέα, and therefore we can and should translate οὐσία, which actually and only denotes beingness, with "essence." This, however, as the general opinion confirms, is not at all obvious, and above all not for us modern and contemporary thinkers.

The reason the Greeks understand essence as whatness is that they in general understand the Being of beings (οὐσία) as what is constant and in its constancy is always present, and as present shows itself, and as self-showing offers its look—in short, as look, as ἰδέα. Only on the basis of this understanding of Being as constant self-opening and self-showing presence is the interpretation of the beingness of beings—hence the interpretation of οὐσία—as ἰδέα possible and necessary.

b) The Greek understanding of the ἰδέα.

In order to ascertain the correct understanding, i.e., the Greek understanding, of the ἰδέα, we must emphasize once more: the ἰδέα—εἶδος—is the look something offers in its "what," the look something exhibits of itself. Why do we stress this?

An objection could immediately be made—especially on the basis of the usual modern modes of thinking—that the characterization of the whatness as ἰδέα precisely does not fulfill what we desired, namely a determination of the whatness in itself. For if the whatness is characterized as something seen, then it is only determined with regard to the way we encounter it and grasp it—with regard to the way it stands over and against us, and not as it is in itself. This possible objection misunderstands the Greek concept of Being, which is precisely self-emerging and self-showing presence. Certainly in the notion of the ἰδέα there resides a relation to ἰδεῖν as a mode of perception. But the perceiving of beings as such is an ἰδεῖν only because a being as such is self-showing: ἰδέα.

Admittedly, we must note here that as soon as the Greek conception of beings as such got lost, i.e., became undetermined, ordinary, and distorted—especially by its translation into the Latin—then the relation of the ἰδέα to ἰδεῖν pushed itself into the foreground. The ἰδέα was no longer understood on the basis of beings and their basic character of presence, but as an image, the counterpart to, and the result of, a particular apprehension and representation. The ἰδέα became a mere representation (*percipere-perceptio*-ἰδέα) and, at the same time, a generalization from the particular (Descartes, nominalism).

The interpretation of Being in terms of presence is the sole reason that for the Greeks the beingness of beings was primarily determined by the whatness. For what a table is as table belongs to every table, whether it be one actually there or one only thought of and wished for. The whatness is the constant. That an individual table, as we say today, "exists," is actual and at hand, this—its reality or existence—does not at all pertain to its essence. From a rigorous Platonic way of thinking, the essence of a being is *impaired* by its entanglement with reality, it loses its purity and so in a certain sense its universality. For example, when the essence "table" is actualized here and now in this specific kind of wood and with these specific dimensions and shape, what is "actual" is only a particular table, and the essence "table" is not thereby fully actual in all its possibilities and variations but is restricted. Thought and seen in the Greek-Platonic way, the single table here and now is certainly not nothing and hence is a being (ὄν), but one which, measured against the essence, is a constriction and therefore properly should not be (μή), a μὴ ὄν. For the Greeks, in the individual things surrounding us and in their relations, what properly is is precisely not the "here and now, such and such," the particular "this" but is, quite to the contrary, the "what" of the individual thing, that which is sighted in advance, the idea. Even Aristotle thinks in this Platonic-Greek mode—despite certain modifications.

Today, however, if a table is real as here and now, then we say it *is*, it "exists," whereas the "idea" is for us something *only* represented and imagined, a mere thought, and precisely not properly real. Therefore for us today "ideas" are worthless if they are not realized. We are interested in realization and success, to such an extent that in the pursuit of success the "ideas" finally get lost. Success as such, however, needs to be augmented by more and more successes, hence by their number and degree. Therefore more velocity is a success, whereas the idea "velocity" remains the same, at most becoming emptier and more worn out.

In Greek thought, this reality of the particular does not belong to the proper and first essence of beings, for that is conceived only as the whatness. The single decisive question as regards the essence is what something is, not whether it exists at hand as an individual. For, this Being as being at hand, real occurrence, means, from the standpoint of the whatness as ἰδέα, something that only accedes to the idea, is accidental, and has no duration. An individual table can be destroyed, and it did not at all exist prior to its fabrication. Insofar as, for the Greeks, Being means constant presence, the beingness of beings (the οὐσία of the ὄν) is determinable only as the whatness in the sense of ἰδέα.

The consequence of this is completely strange to our way of thinking, namely that for the Greeks the "existence" and reality of beings, hence precisely what we are wont to denote as the "Being" of beings, does not at all belong to the beingness of beings. Hence in the course of Western history since the time of the Greeks, there must have occurred a reversal in the conception of "Being," whose import we still do not suspect and appreciate, because we continue to stumble on quite thoughtlessly in the aftermath of this reversal. The reversal in the conception of Being is all the more enigmatic in that it came to pass entirely within the framework and on the basis of the interpretation of Being first acquired by the Greeks themselves.

To the extent that even today we still ask about the essence in the traditional way, we are asking about the whatness and are excluding the presence at hand, the reality, of the individual being. We are in a way then asking about the ἰδέα, though in the sense of the κοινόν, the universal. Yet even in this conception of the essence there is implied an abstraction from the individual being as here and now, such and such.

§19. *The absence of a foundation for Aristotle's essential determination of truth as the correctness of an assertion. The question of the meaning of foundation.*

We are now better prepared for the question that occasioned these deliberations about the essence as such. The questions is: how does Aristotle found the essential determination of truth in the sense of the correctness of an assertion? Why does the whatness of truth reside in the correctness of an assertion? To what extent is the correctness of an assertion the "idea" of truth and consequently the universal that pertains to everything true as such?

The first step will be to look about in Aristotle himself and see how he founds this essence of truth and its positing. And here a remarkable thing appears: no foundation is given. The essential determination of truth is simply proclaimed. What is true is that representing and meaning and saying which is ὅμοιον, similar, corresponding, to the πράγματα; and the false is what is ἐναντίως ἢ τὰ πράγματα.[1] What can be true or false, what proves to be the seat of this possibility and consequently the locus of truth as conformity and correctness, is the λόγος, the assertion, the asserting thought: οὐ γάρ ἐστι τὸ ψεῦδος καὶ τὸ ἀληθὲς ἐν τοῖς πράγμασιν, . . . ἀλλ' ἐν διανοίᾳ.[2] That here it is said explicitly of the truth: οὐκ ἐν τοῖς πράγμασιν ["It is not in the things"—Tr.] may be a hint that it does *precisely* belong there in a certain, and perhaps more original, way.

One might try to vindicate this fact, that the essential determination of truth as the correctness of an assertion is not founded but only proclaimed, by having recourse to the pretense that the trea-

1. *Cf.* Aristotle, *Metaphysica*, Θ 10. ["At odds with the things"—Tr.]
2. Aristotle, *Metaphysica*, E 4, 1027b 25ff. ["For falsity and truth do not lie in the things . . . but in the mind"–Tr.]

tises containing the foundation have been lost. For it is certainly not possible to assume a thinker of Aristotle's rank would simply proclaim arbitrarily and without foundation such a decisive determination as that of the essence of truth. And yet no reference is ever made to such treatises in which the foundation would be supplied. Quite to the contrary, the foundation we are seeking should be discovered, if anywhere, precisely where Aristotle deals with truth as a property of the assertion (*Met.* E 4, *Met.* Θ 10, *De anima* Γ, *De interpretatione*), and it is exactly there that we look in vain.

Yet we will be able to think through and appreciate the full import of the fact that there is no genuine foundation given to this positing of the essence of truth as the correctness of an assertion only if we realize that since in general the traditional conception of truth is not founded, the state of everything true that we seek, find, and establish in the light of this essential determination must be very remarkable. All this is true and correct—on the basis of an unfounded opinion about truth: true on a basis which is not a basis at all and which will one day come to light in its groundlessness, even if only very slowly and only visible for very few.

But before we decide to draw such a conclusion, we must once more critically examine the question at stake here. The positing of the essence of truth as the correctness of an assertion is obviously only *one* essential determination among others. For Plato's philosophy, and Aristotle's, also determine the essence of the soul, motion, place, time, friendship, justice, the state, man, etc. What is at issue in each case is, Platonically speaking, the determination of "ideas," and in each case a genuine foundation is lacking. Perhaps under the title "foundation" we are seeking something which may not be sought and demanded regarding an essential determination. Then would what is essential in the knowledge of and comportment toward beings, the view in advance of the "idea," the determination of the essence, be groundless and arbitrary?

So it is now time to ask precisely how we are to understand "founding." To found an assertion means to indicate its ground, to exhibit the basis of its legitimacy, of its correctness. Consequently, to found in the genuine sense is to exhibit and show that about which the assertion says something. This must be the standard to measure whether what is said is appropriate to the thing (correct). The assertion "Lecture hall number five of the classroom building of Freiburg is now occupied" is founded in that way only if we demonstrate what is said through immediate perception. This fact of the occupancy of the lecture hall is brought before our eyes, i.e., we bring ourselves before it—as that in which the assertion has its support. There is certainly no kind of foundation with a higher certitude, and it is therefore that each factual proof makes an impression on everyone. The assertion "There is now snow on the Feldberg" will thus be demonstrated as correct by our wandering up there and perceiving the fact with our own eyes. But we can also let the weather station give us the information. This foundation is already a mediate one, not only because we are not ourselves ascertaining this claim by means of demonstration, but because we must here presuppose that the weather station is providing correct information, that we ourselves are hearing correctly, that in general the telephone transmission is in order, etc. These are all presuppositions which are by no means self-evident, but which we tacitly assume to be reliable in our factual knowledge. But of course we know that immediate proof by means of an object present at hand is rightly to be preferred.

Now, as we saw, a knowledge of the essence precedes in a certain way all other cognizing, confirming, and founding. To walk around in a house—using this simple example again—and the particular modes of comportment included in inhabiting a house would not be possible at all if we were not guided by a cognition of house-ness, i.e., of *what* a house is. Consequently, that which sustains and guides all particular cognitions and comportment, namely the knowledge of the essence, must, in accord with its sustaining and guiding function, be founded all the more. Its founding, in conformity with its rank, will claim the highest possible mode of foundation.

RECAPITULATION

1) The conception of the Being of beings as constant presence: the ground for the determination of the essence (ἰδέα) as whatness.

We are asking: How does Greek philosophy found that determination of the essence of truth which since the time of the Greeks has sustained and guided Western thought and knowledge up to the present day? As a preparation for the answer to this question we needed to elucidate how the Greeks delimited the essentiality of the essence. The essence of whatever we encounter, of whatever is given, is the ἰδέα. What is perplexing in this characterization of the essence as idea becomes more understandable if we consider that the essence of something means what it *is* and that consequently a determinate conception of the Being of beings is founding and must be so.

The Greeks understand by Being the constant presence of something. What is constant in any particular being is its what-it-is, and what is present is precisely this "what" as the being's prevailing look, εἶδος. Thus it is also intelligible why "reality," being at hand, does not properly belong to beings, for what something is can also exist in possibility. A possible table *is* indeed a table; it has this whatness even if the table is not present at hand. The realization of the essence is in a certain sense accidental to the essence, and at the same time is an impairment of the pure essence, for in a real table only one possibility is realized.

Insofar as we today are accustomed to consider as a being in the most genuine sense precisely what happens to be here and now, a particular individuation or instance of being present at hand, and apply the word "Being" primarily to reality and presence at hand, a transformation must have been accomplished over and against the Greek conception of Being, one to which in this context we can only refer. In relation to the essence as whatness, the presence at hand of a particular individuation of the essence is of no importance to the Greeks. To keep this in mind is crucial for the following question.

2) The absence of a foundation for the positing and for the characterization of the essence of truth as the correctness of an assertion. The meaning of foundation.

We are now asking how the Greeks, and that also means later thinking, founded the positing of the essence of anything. More precisely and more closely related to our inquiry: how did Aristotle found his original characterization of the essence of truth as the correctness of an assertion? We look in vain for a foundation.

And because other essential assertions are just as little founded, the absence of a foundation for the definition of truth cannot be explained by saying that the pertinent treatise was perhaps not handed down to us.

But what sort of perspective is opened up here? Are the essence of truth and the positing of the essence supposed to be unfounded, and consequently is all concern for truth basically groundless? Is it a mere accident that the foundation of the essential determination of truth is absent, or is a foundation impossible here? What does "founding" mean in this case and in general? We clarified what it first means with the example of an assertion about something given here and now. "The lights in this lecture hall are now on"—this assertion is founded through perception, simply by referring to the "fact." This kind of proof through the exhibition of the very presence of what is named is obviously the safest and most immediate way by which we can provide an assertion the ground upon which what is said in it rests, assuming it does coincide with what is exhibited. As we saw, however, insofar as the view in advance of the essence and a "knowledge" of the essence guide and dominate all experience and all comportment to beings, this ruling knowledge of the essence, in accord with its rank, must also claim the highest possible mode of demonstration. But there is no higher mode of demonstration than immediate reference to the corresponding given things.

Chapter Three

The Laying of the Ground as the Foundation for Grasping an Essence

§20. *The absurdity of attempting to found an essential statement about truth as correctness by having recourse to a factual statement.*

Our concern is the founding of the essential determination of truth as the correctness of an assertion. The statement "Truth is the correctness of an assertion" can be sufficiently proven only by the exhibition of an actual correct assertion, a true statement, as a fact, e.g., the statement we gave about the lecture hall. This statement is a true one. Through it, as a true statement, the essence of the truth must be demonstrable:

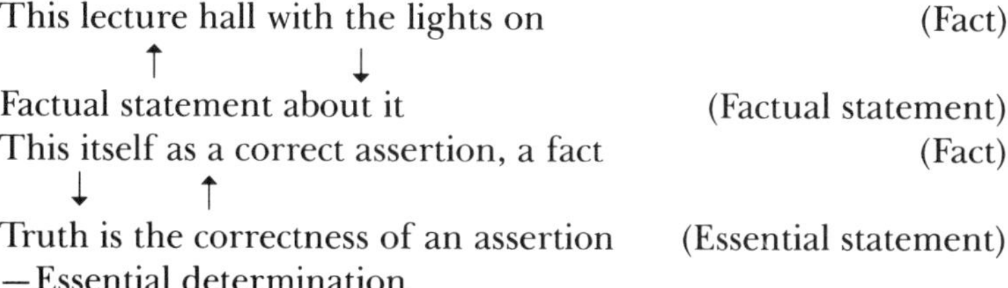

But we must have already realized that the appeal to the *fact* of a single correct assertion can never demonstrate that the *essence* of truth is the correctness of an assertion. At most, it is the other way around: we could get the idea of offering a particular assertion as an example of the essence of truth, and hence as an instance of "truth," only if it was already established and founded in advance that truth means the correctness of an assertion. We are not seeking here the foundation of an assertion about individual facts (e.g., the present occupancy of this lecture hall); we are seeking the foundation of a determination of the *essence* of truth. The essence does not mean a single case; its distinction is to be valid for many. The determination of the essence of truth applies to *all* correct assertions. Consequently the essential determination of truth as the correctness of an assertion can only be demonstrated by exhibiting *all* actual assertions, so that the accordance of the essential delimitation would be demonstrated for each and every one of them.

But how in the world could Aristotle present himself with all actually performed assertions—his own as well as all those of others, past and future—in order to demonstrate thereby the legitimacy of an essential determination of truth? That is obviously impossible. Hence it follows that an essential determination cannot be proved by facts (in our case by factually performed correct assertions)—in the first place because these facts cannot at all be surveyed and exhibited. And even if this futility were successful, the essential determination would still not be grounded. For the essence applies not only to all actual assertions, but likewise and a fortiori to all possible assertions, ones which might never be performed. But how could anyone demonstrate the appropriateness of the definition of the essence of truth to possible cases of correct assertions? Therefore, the way we founded the assertion about this lecture hall (its factual occupancy), as a factual statement, is not how the essential statement, "Truth is the correctness of an assertion," can be founded. And indeed this is so not only because neither the factual nor the possible cases can all be exhibited without exception, but primarily because this way of founding—demonstrating an essential assertion by recourse to single corresponding instances—is altogether absurd. Supposing we wanted to prove the essential assertion in its legitimacy by adducing correct propositions, in order to measure the appropriateness to them of the essential assertion and to find that it corresponds to them, that truth is the correctness of a proposition, how could we find those correct propositions which are supposed to serve as proofs for the legitimacy of the essential determination? Indeed, we could do so only if we separated them from false propositions, and we could do that only if we already knew in advance what true propositions are, that is, only if we already knew what their truth consists in. Every time we attempt to prove an essential determination through single, or even all, actual and possible facts, there results the remarkable state of affairs that we have already presupposed the legitimacy of the essential determination, indeed must presuppose it, just in order to grasp and produce the facts that are supposed to serve as proof.

§21. *Grasping the essence as bringing it forth. First directive.*

Accordingly, the foundation of an essential statement possesses its own peculiarity and its own difficulty. The grasping of the essence and consequently the foundation of the positing of the essence are of another kind than the cognition of single facts and factual nexuses, and correspondingly different from the foundation of such factual cognition. In order to see more clearly here, we will deliberate further on a single case.

How could the essence "table," what a table is, be determined and set forth at all if we did not encounter in advance at least one single real table, on the basis of which—by means of so-called "abstraction"—we draw out and read off the general essence "table" and disregard the particularities of any individual table? But then again, we have to ask, where would this one single table—as table—come from if the idea of what a table is in general were not already guiding its very fabrication and realization? Must the idea "table" not be brought forth in advance even for the first of all tables to be crafted? Or do both of these go hand in hand? In any case, is the grasping of the essence not of such a kind that, as grasping, in a certain sense it first "brings forth" the essence and does not somehow patch it together subsequently, out of already present at hand single cases?

But according to what law and rule is the "bringing forth" of the essence accomplished? Is it an arbitrary product of thought, which is then supplied with a word? Is everything a matter of pure arbitrariness here? If not, is it then perhaps only a question of linguistic convention? That is, perhaps everyone agrees to use certain words as signs for definite representations and to connect the word "table" with the representation of this particular thing. What is common is then only the sameness of the word "table," used to denote any individual table. Furthermore, there is nothing like the unity and sameness of an essence corresponding to the *one* word "table"; the whole question of essence comes down to a matter of grammar. There are only individual tables, and beyond them there is no such thing as an "essence" table. What is called that way is, from a critical standpoint, only the sameness of the sign for naming individual tables, the only real ones.

But precisely that which characterizes the table as table—that which it is and distinguishes it in its whatness from the window—is in a certain manner independent of the word and the linguistic formations. For the word of another language is different phonetically and orthographically and yet it means the same thing, "table." This "one and the same" first provides purpose and consistency to the agreement in linguistic usage. Accordingly, the essence must have already been posited in advance, in order to be signifiable and expressible as the same in the same word. Perhaps genuine naming and saying constitute an original positing of the essence, although certainly not by means of agreement and convention but through *dominating speech*, which provides the standard. At all events, the essence does not at all tolerate a subsequent deduction—neither from the agreement in linguistic usage nor from a comparison of individual cases.

§22. *The search for the ground of the positing of the essence. Ordinariness of an acquaintance with the essence—enigma of a genuine knowledge of the essence (grasping of the essence) and its foundation.*

We are seeking what gives the positing of the essence its ground and its legitimacy, in order to rescue it from arbitrariness. In all these reflections we encounter again and again the same thing: that a grasping of the essence (as well as a mere acquaintance with the essence) is already what provides legitimacy and a standard; accordingly, it is something original, and thus, for ordinary thinking and its demands for foundation, something uncommon and strange.

We cannot dwell on this strangeness too often and too long. Therefore we will reflect anew on what occurs within the realm of our acquaintance with the essence. To say it briefly in advance: acquaintance with the essence is for us as ordinary and necessary as genuine knowledge of the essence appears to be enigmatic and arbitrary. We are acquainted with the "essence" of the things surrounding us: house, tree, bird, road, vehicle, man, etc., and yet we have no knowledge of the essence. For we immediately land in the uncertain, shifting, controversial, and groundless, when we attempt to determine more closely, and above all try to ground in its determinateness, what is certainly though still indeterminately "known": namely, house-ness, tree-ness, birdness, humanness. On the other hand, we are able to distinguish these things very well, so that we do not confuse a bird with a house. This acquaintance with the essence—no matter how preliminary and undetermined, no matter how used up and worn it might be—guides us constantly and everywhere at every step and every dwelling place in the midst of beings and in every thought about them. This remarkable state of affairs indicates that it is not the immediately given facts—the individual real, graspable, and visible things, precisely those that are intended and acquired—that possess the decisive "closeness" to "life." More close to life, to use this way of speaking, closer than so-called "reality," is the essence of things, which we know and yet do not know. What is close and closest is not what the so-called "man of facts" thinks he grasps; instead, the closest is the essence, which admittedly remains for the many the farthest of all—even when it is explicitly shown to them, insofar as it allows itself to be shown in the usual way at all.

What kind of enigma are we encountering here? What sort of mystery overtakes man such that what to him seem to be beings pure and simple—facts, so famously close to reality—are not what beings are, that nevertheless this constant ignoring of the closeness of the essence of beings belongs perhaps still to the essence of man, and that this ignoring precisely therefore may not be evaluated as a lack but must be understood as the necessary condition for the possible greatness of man: that he dwells in between Being and appearance and that for him what is closest is the farthest and what is farthest is closest? What kind of great upheaval here strikes man and his place within beings?

If every relation of man to the essence of beings is so enigmatic, it is no wonder that it is only in slow and ever slipping and halting steps that we come to understand the grasping of the essence, the foundation of the grasping of the essence, and consequently the knowledge of the essence and its relation to mere acquaintance with the essence. In view of this great upheaval in man we will see more clearly that and why all great epochs of history became great and remained great because they possessed the strength to experience this upheaval and to sustain it, i.e., to collapse under it in such a way that the fragments of this collapse became nothing else than the essential works and deeds of these epochs. We must always think out toward these things if we do not want to lapse into the catastrophical and usual error of believing that the question "How do we grasp the essence and how do we found the grasping of it?" is an "abstract" and "intellectual" playing with concepts, for "intellectualism" consists precisely in the opinion that the "facts" are the sole reality and the only beings.

§23. *The bringing of the essence into view in advance (the grasping of the essence) as the bringing forth of the essence out of concealment into the light. The productive seeing of the essence.*

The result of our reflection up to now is that the essence is not gleaned from facts and is never to be found as a fact. If the essence nevertheless stands before us in the view in advance, what else can that mean but that in some way it is brought before us and we bring ourselves before the essence?

The grasping of the essence is a kind of bringing forth of the essence. The way of "founding" the essence and positing it must also have a corresponding form. For if, in the grasping of the essence, that which is to be grasped is first brought forth, and if consequently the grasping as such is a bringing forth, then the "foundation" of the grasping cannot be an appeal to something already present at hand to which the grasping would be assimilated. Compared to such a foundation—i.e., the demonstration by means of something already pregiven in the manner of the foundation of all knowledge of facts—the knowledge of the essence is therefore necessarily unfounded. But are we then to conclude that the knowledge of the essence is groundless?

In order to come to an answer here, we must try to determine more precisely how the grasping of the essence, as a bringing forth of the essence, comes to pass. Corresponding to the direction taken by our question about the essentiality of the essence, we must here again ask how the Greeks, following *their* conception of the essence, understand and must understand this "bringing forth."

Plato characterizes the essence as the whatness of a being and the whatness as ἰδέα, the look a being shows of itself. Any individual being is produced and comes properly to a stand in *what* it is. The "*what* it is" posits the being in itself and on itself; it is its form. What an individual being, e.g., a table is—its look, its form, and hence its structure—is not gleaned from already present at hand individual tables, but rather the reverse, these individual tables can be fabricated and be present at hand as ready-made, only if, and insofar as, they are produced following the exemplar of something like a table in general. The exemplar is the look which is sighted in advance, the look of that which makes up the outer aspect of the table—the "idea," the essence.

But is this advance sight, the bringing into sight of the essence, supposed to be a "bringing forth"? Everything speaks against it. In order to bring something into sight, must not that which is to be glimpsed already exist? To be sure. Thus at least the Greek-Platonic conception of the essence as ἰδέα excludes the notion that the grasping of the essence is a bringing forth of the essence. It has been well known for ages that, according to the usual conception of the Platonic doctrine of the ideas, Plato taught that the ideas would exist—untouched by all change and perishing—for themselves and in themselves, in a place above the heavens, to the point that it would be wholly un-Greek to say that the ideas would be brought forth.

Nevertheless, the grasping of the essence is indeed, even for the Greeks, a bringing forth. To see that we must only understand "bringing forth" in the Greek manner. The "bringing forth" of the essence, according to our preceding reflections, means first of all and polemically that the essence is not gleaned from the individual cases as their universal; it has its own origin. When we today speak of bringing forth, we think of the making and fabricating of an individual object. But this is precisely what is not intended; bringing forth—we use this expression intentionally—must be taken here quite literally. The essence is brought forth, brought out from its previous obscurity and hiddenness. Forth—into what? Into the light; it is brought into view. This bringing into view is a peculiar seeing. This seeing does not see by merely staring at what is present at hand or what is otherwise already accessible, but instead this seeing first brings before itself that which is to be seen. It is a seeing that draws something forth, not a mere looking at what is standing about waiting for people to come across as they go their way. It is not a mere noticing of something previously unheeded though otherwise observable without further ado. The seeing of the look that is called the idea is a seeing which draws forth, a seeing which in the very act of seeing compels what is to be seen before itself. Therefore we call this seeing, which first brings forth into visibility that which is to be seen, and produces it before itself, "productive seeing" [*Er-sehen*].[1]

This bringing forth or producing is not a fabricating or a making; hence it is indeed a coming across something. What we can come across must already lie before us. For the Greeks, "Being" means constant presence, and therefore the essence, the whatness, is the most genuine of beings, the being-est of beings, ὄντως ὄν. Therefore the ideas *are*; indeed, they must *be*, as the most proper beings of all beings, in order to be able to be brought forth and put into the light, into the light in which that eye sees which casts views in advance. And it is in the circle of these views that we first grasp individual beings. The productive seeing of the essence is consequently not a conformity to some-

1. ["Productive" is to be understood here in the sense in which, e.g., witnesses are "produced" in court—they are not created for the occasion but simply led forth, literally "pro-duced."—Tr.]

thing otherwise already available but the putting forth of the look—a productive looking in an emphatic sense of the word.

For the Greeks, the essence and the positing of the essence thus stand within a peculiar twilight: the essence is not manufactured, but it is also not simply encountered like a thing already present at hand. Instead, it is brought forth in a productive seeing. Whence and whither? Out of invisibility into the visible, out of what is unthought into what is henceforth to be thought. The productive seeing of the idea, of the essence, is therefore an original way of grasping, and to it must also correspond its own proper way of foundation.

§24. *The productive seeing of the essence as the laying of the ground.* Ὑπόθεσις *as* θέσις *of the* ὑποκείμενον.

Then what about the foundation of the grasping of the essence, which is the actual focus of our question? If this grasping is a productive seeing, a bringing forth, it cannot conform itself to something already present at hand in order to glean information from it, because it is indeed the productive seeing that brings forth the essence in the first place and consequently is that from which the conformity must take direction. In productive seeing, a conformity to something pregiven is not possible, because the productive seeing itself first brings about the pregivenness.

Since here an adequation to what is pregiven is not possible, and is not necessary, there can also not be a foundation in the sense we spoke of earlier. The productive seeing of the essence is not founded, but it is grounded, i.e., accomplished in such a way that it brings itself upon the ground which it itself lays. The productive seeing of the essence is itself the laying of the ground—the positing of what is to be the ground, ὑποκείμενον. The productive seeing as the foundational bringing forth of the essence as ἰδέα is therefore ὑπόθεσις—positing the whatness itself as the ground.

Ὑπόθεσις means here the θέσις of the ὑποκείμενον and has nothing in common with the later concept of "hypothesis," namely an assumption made to guide an experiment and give it a particular direction. All hypotheses in the modern sense—e.g., working hypotheses in natural science—already presuppose the positing of a determinate essence of the beings aimed at, and on the ground of this essence the working hypotheses first get their sense. Every "hypothesis" presupposes a ὑπόθεσις, a prior positing of the essence. The productive seeing of the essence is the positing of the ground; it grounds itself in what it brings forth and it brings forth that in which it grounds itself.

The positing of the essence will therefore always appear arbitrary and unusual if measured against the standards of the usual and familiar. But this unfamiliarity is again not what is remote and peculiar; on the contrary, it is the simple—which can never be brought closer, no matter how many demonstrations are attempted, if it is not brought forth anew in productive seeing, i.e., if the view of the essence is not awakened in man.

Here we see something of the unfathomable distinction between philosophy, as the knowledge of the essence, and all science. Scientific cognition needs, and creates, distance from its object, which is the reason a subsequent technical-practical removal of the distance is necessary. The knowledge of the essence, conversely, creates precisely an appurtenance to Being, and all practical application comes too late and remains beneath the rank of this knowledge.

The knowledge of the essence, therefore, if it is to be shared, must itself be accomplished anew by the one who is to assume it. More precisely, it cannot be communicated in the sense of the passing on of a proposition, whose content is simply grasped without its foundation and its acquisition being accomplished again. The knowledge of the essence must be accomplished anew by each one who is to share it; it must genuinely be co-accomplished.

RECAPITULATION

1) Renewed reflection on our procedure as a whole: the necessity of a historical relation to the history of the essence of truth.

Before we briefly recall the previous course of our questioning, in order to carry it on, let us characterize anew our procedure as a whole. I say "anew," because a clarification of it was already attempted in what has preceded—namely in the interpolated discussions of the distinction between historiographical consideration and historical reflection. Why did we focus on precisely this distinction, one that concerns a basic attitude within history and toward history? Why did a discussion of history and historiography become necessary at all for the sake of a clarification of our procedure? Why?—because we are asking the question of the essence of truth.

Questions such as that one pertain to the construction of a "system of philosophy" and are called, according to this origin, "systematic," in distinction to the "historiographical" reports about the philosophical opinions of other thinkers on an issue. We are asking a systematic question—even if we have no system in mind—insofar as we are asking from ourselves and for ourselves, and for the future. We are questioning systematically and yet, after taking only a few steps with this intention, we have lost ourselves in historiographical considerations. Is this not a duplicitous procedure, a detour, even an avoidance of the simple, immediate, and direct answering of the question we raised: what is the essence of truth? One could perhaps understand that our response to this question might necessitate a certain historiographical account of the theories of truth immediately preceding us, for the purpose of critical analysis and clarification. But why go back so far and so laboriously to the Greeks?

If, as appears to be the case, we are already raising the question more originally than ever before and intend to answer in the same way, why do we not then leave behind everything bygone; why not simply throw off the oppressing and confusing burden of the tradition, in order finally to begin for ourselves? This is certainly what we intend and we *must* do so, since—as will be shown—there is a necessity behind it. But what we must do here—overcome the historiographical tradition—we can do only on the basis of the deepest and most genuine *historical* relation to what we have put into question, namely truth and the history of its essence.

Let us deliberate a moment: how could it happen that Western man, and especially modern man, became so inundated and shaken by the historiographical transmission of objectively and temporally very diverse modes of thinking and evaluating, styles of creating, and forms of work that he became vacillating as to his essence and is now the hodgepodge he is today? Why is man so defenselessly exposed to the constant assault of the historiographical? Why?—because Western man is historical in his essence, i.e., he is founding of history and at the same time destructive of it. Where man lives without history, historiography cannot become meaningful for him and hence cannot possibly gain power over him. Historiography, however, did not gain this confusing ascendancy over contemporary man, to an extent we can hardly imagine, because man has become *too* historical, but, quite to the contrary, it is because man is no longer historical enough in an original way and so cannot set limits to historiography and assign it its proper end.

We can therefore defend ourselves against the inundations of historiography (today the tide is rising higher and higher) only by, as it were, jumping out of history, although we will gain domination over historiography solely by winning back the power to take up historical Being. The loss of this power is neither accidental nor an isolated process. Instead, it belongs together most intimately with that event in Western history which Hölderlin was the first to suffer and thereby genuinely experience, and which Nietzsche subsequently expressed in his own way, by pointing out that Western man has, for the last two millennia, been unable to fashion for himself a God. What is the meaning of this lack of the power to fashion a God? We do not know. But it would be a much too cheap account if we deduced from it already the decline of Western man, even if it appears that all the powers of the West still at work, perhaps also those of the earth, are submerged in the pursuit and production of what is closest and most palpable, i.e., of what is useful to the many and to the life-will of anyone at all. History does not withhold itself from prediction but from calculating judgment, especially if we understand history in its longest and hence slowest and therefore hardly graspable occurrence: namely, the approach and distantiation of the gods in relation to beings—an event which lies far beyond and well on this side of the facticities of religions and churches and cults and which has as its concomitant opposite side what we are calling man's strength or lack of strength with regard to history.

If there once were gods, who are now in flight from man, as they have been for ages, then this self-refusal of the gods must be a terrible occurrence, which surely sets in motion a singular event which we may hardly risk naming. (Unsaid: the passing of the last god. Cf: *Vom Ereignis* ["On the Appropriating Event"].) Whether we think forth to this occurrence, or ponder the sagging strength of man with regard to history, or think through both these in their original connection—in each case reflection encounters the one and only basic character of this most original and most concealed, but also most genuine, history: that truth in its essence is no longer a question but instead possesses a prosaic obviousness and thereby uproots everything true and has no creative power. Truth will never again become a question arising out of a genuine necessity as long as we are unable to recall what its beginning essence was, i.e., where its future essence must be decided.

The question of the essence of truth is an—indeed *the*—utterly historical question, insofar as it asks about what restores our history to its ground in the first place, i.e., asks about that from which the unavoidable and the decidable gain the space of their conflict and of their reciprocal self-surpassing.

Our question about the essence of truth immediately arrives on the path of a historical reflection, and indeed of one reaching back very far, and has therein, according to the intention of our lectures, its genuine import. But that is exactly what is required—if we reflect on what has been said—by our inquiry into the essence of truth itself, which does not only "have" its history for itself but is in ever different ways the ground and the absence of ground of our history and of our absence of history. In future thinking, the distinction between historiographical and systematic considerations will lose all meaning—completely different from the case of Hegel, who only mixed them up and had to let them both exist in disarray.

2) The succession of the steps made up to now from truth as the correctness of an assertion to the positing of the essence as a productive seeing and a laying of the ground.

But because this historical interrogation is required by what is interrogated itself, we can and should arrive at the attempted historical reflection only by means of a rigorous sequence of steps of genuine questioning. Let us once more briefly characterize the sequence of steps taken up to now.

Our question about the essence of truth began with the determination of truth as the correctness of an assertion or, in general, of a representation, a determination which still today provides the standard and has done so for two millennia. This beginning was executed immediately in the form of a critical reflection. The result was the following: truth as correctness of representing presupposes, in order to be what it is (assimilation to the object), the openness of beings by which they become capable of being ob-jects in the first place and by which the representing becomes a faculty of presenting something before itself as such. This openness appeared consequently as the ground of the possibility of correctness. Accordingly, correctness cannot constitute the original essence of truth if it itself is dependent on something more original. The original essence of truth must then be sought in a return to this openness.

But this simple critical reflection, which transcends the traditional concept of truth, is tenable only if correctness already contains in some way, even if not originally, something of the essence of truth. That it does so was at first only tacitly presupposed. What about this presupposition? How and to what extent is the traditional positing of the essence of truth as the correctness of an assertion founded? We will discover, if at all, the foundation of this essential determination of truth in an immediate way where this essence of truth was established for the first time. That happened at the end of the great philosophy of the Greeks, in the thinking of Plato and in the doctrines of Aristotle.

But in order now to interrogate with certitude the legitimacy of the essential determination of truth as correctness, we have to know what those thinkers intended by what we call "essence." This led to the exposition of what Plato understood as ἰδέα. The essence is the whatness of a being, understood as its look or countenance, which is kept in view in advance for every comportment toward the individual being present at hand. If now, after this elucidation of the Greek concept of essence, we examine in which way the just-mentioned determination of the essence of truth—as the correctness of an assertion—is founded, then we discover that a "foundation" is lacking. The positings of the essence appear to be arbitrary declarations, to which, however, we acquiesce. The positings of the essence are without foundation if we understand by "foundation" the always subsequent reference back of what is asserted to something already purely and simply present at hand, even if not always known. The only knowledge that can be demonstrated in such a way, hence that can be founded, is one which tries to know and determine what is present at hand, i.e., a knowledge of facts. In all factual knowledge, however, there already resides an essential knowledge guiding and supporting it. The result of these reflections was that a grasping of the essence can never be founded through a knowledge of facts. For in the first place all real factual particularizations of the essence in question—e.g., the essence of a table—can never be collected, and secondly, this gathering would still be insufficient, since the essence also holds for *possible* instances. Thirdly, and above all, the notion of a foundation of the essence and of the determination of the essence by reference to corresponding real and possible facts is in itself absurd. For in order to discover the facts pertaining to the essence and to select them and exhibit them as justifications for the legitimacy of this positing of the essence, the positing of the essence must already be presupposed.

Consequently, the essence and the determination of the essence do not admit any foundation of the kind that we accomplish in the field of factual knowledge. The essence of something is not at all to be discovered simply like a fact; on the contrary, it must be *brought forth*, since it is not directly present in the sphere of immediate representing and intending. To bring forth is a kind of making, and so there resides in all grasping and positing of the essence something creative. The creative always appears violent and arbitrary, as if it should be concealed that it is bound to a higher lawfulness which must be protected against the intrusion of common opinion. For the latter has its own rules, puts them into play everywhere, and abhors the exception. If we call the positing of the essence a bringing-forth and thereby first of all take "essence" according to the Greek conception (ἰδέα), then the "bringing-forth" must also be understood in the Greek sense.

To bring forth means to bring out into the light, to bring something in sight which was up to then not seen at all, and specifically such that the seeing of it is not simply a gaping at something already lying there but a seeing which, in seeing, first brings forth what is to be seen, i.e., a productive seeing. The essence, i.e., the Greek-Platonic ἰδέα, the look of beings in what they are, is grasped in such a productive seeing. The philosopher is a thinker only if he is this kind of seer and not a gaper or a calculator or a mere babbler. Every "foundation" in the sense we discussed comes too late with regard to the positing of the essence, because the productive seeing of the essence is itself a productive seeing of that in which the essence has its ground—a productive seeing of what its ground is. Knowledge of the essence is in itself a ground-laying. It is the positing of what lies under as ground, the positing of the ὑποκείμενον—θέσις—and hence is ὑπόθεσις. It is not the subsequent adding of a ground for something already represented. When a thing is determined as to its essence, then this essence itself is productively seen. The productive seeing of the essence brings something into view for the essence and claims it for the essence, out of which it—the essence—becomes visible for what it is.

§25. *The unconcealedness of the whatness of beings as the truth pertaining to the grasping of the essence. The groundedness of the correctness of an assertion in unconcealedness* (ἀλήθεια).

We now have to apply what has been said to the question occupying us about the "foundation" of the traditional positing of the essence of truth as the correctness of an assertion.

Knowledge of an essence cannot be founded in the strict sense of foundation (demonstration by appeal to something present at hand). It is not, however, on that account groundless but is itself a ground-laying. Consequently, it is no accident that we do not find in Aristotle a foundation for the positing of the essence of truth as the correctness of an assertion; it is necessarily so, because there is no foundation for the positing of an essence. On the other hand, however, we can now at least surmise that this determination of the essence of truth as the correctness of an assertion is not arbitrary and groundless but is itself a grounding, the laying of a ground and thereby a return to the ground. We will therefore ask: What does this Aristotelian, and now usual, determination of truth as the correctness of an assertion claim as its ground? What does this determination of the essence of truth see and have in view in advance as that wherein it finds itself grounded? To arrive at the answer we will intentionally make a brief detour.

Earlier (pp. 28 ff., 35 f.), we came to a point in our considerations where we had to say that the philosophical question about the essence of truth is at the same time and in itself the question of the truth of the essence. This relation also holds in the converse: the question of the truth of the essence is at the same time a question about the essence of truth. These statements appear at first to be mere conjectures. But we have now progressed far enough to make them evident in their truth—even if only in the compass of a restricted field of view.

We are asking about the essence of truth or, more precisely, about the Aristotelian determination of the essence of truth as the correctness of an assertion: in *what* is this determination of the essence itself grounded? The question of the essence of truth is—still conjecturally—the question of the truth of essence. The result of our questioning the essentiality of the essence was that the essence is the whatness of something, the ἰδέα, the look something offers, its appearance, the being in its being-viewed. A productive seeing grasps the ἰδέα. The productive seeing is a bringing-forth, a bringing into the light, a bringing into visibility, which is itself grounded on what it brings forth and in that way posits what is seen as ground—ὑπόθεσις.

The productive seeing of the essence does not admit any foundation; that would be, so to say, beneath its dignity. For what actually is "founding"? It is an appeal to something present at hand, and that implies the measuring of the cognition or of the assertion against something pre-given, to which the assertion and the representation are to conform. Founding is a conformity to . . . . Founding consequently presupposes in itself and for itself the possibility of conformity and correctness. Founding and the possibility of being founded are tied to a determinate kind of truth, namely the correctness of representation and assertion. Only what is correct and what claims correctness can be founded and is in need of foundation.

Now if all grasping and positing of the essence exclude the possibility of being founded—not because the foundation cannot be discovered, but because founding as such is not sufficient for the legitimation of the positing of an essence—if the grasping of the essence rejects every attempt at a foundation in the sense we discussed, then the truth which belongs to the grasping of the essence and which is stamped on it cannot be correctness. Therefore another kind of truth must belong to the grasping of the essence. Thus a reflection on the truth of essence, on what a grasping of essence is, and what its justification is, becomes a reflection on the essence of truth.

The grasping of the essence is a bringing-forth: specifically, in the Greek sense of a bringing out and fetching forth. Whence? From concealment. Whither? Into unconcealedness, in order to posit it as the unconcealed. To see the essence in productive seeing means to posit the unconcealed of beings, to posit beings in their unconcealedness, to take them up into the naming word, and in that way establish them and thereby let them stand in the visibility of an essential cognition.

The unconcealed is in Greek τὸ ἀληθές, and unconcealedness is ἀλήθεια. For ages, this has been translated as *veritas*, "truth" [*Wahrheit*]. The "truth" of the grasping of the essence is, thought in the Greek manner, the unconcealedness of the whatness of beings. Unconcealedness, the being-seen of beings is, in Platonic terms, ἰδέα.

A being in its beingness (οὐσία) is, briefly and properly, the unconcealedness of the being itself. Beings, determined with regard to their unconcealedness, are thereby grasped with respect to their coming forth and emerging, their φύσις, i.e., as ἰδέα, and so are grasped as nothing other than beings in their beingness. To productively see a being as such in its beingness—in what it is as a being—means nothing else than to encounter it simply in its unconcealedness, and, as Aristotle (*Met.* Θ 10) says, θιγεῖν, to feel it, simply touch upon it and in touching it to push it forward, to bring it before oneself, to produce and see its look. Since, in the Greek experience, beings as such are φύσις, emergence, there belongs to beings as such ἀλήθεια, unconcealedness. Therefore the grasping of beings as such must be a disclosing (a taking out from concealment). We cannot now articulate more precisely what all this signifies in a more profound sense and in every one of its consequences, namely that for the Greeks the truth is a—indeed, *the*—character of beings as such. We will only note that the grasping of the essence claims a special kind of "truth": unconcealedness.

As we have heard often enough, all cognition and knowledge of individual beings is grounded in an acquaintance with the essence. Knowledge as the representation of individual beings is founded to the extent that it is correct. Now, however, if the knowledge of individual beings, the true representing of facts, is grounded in a knowledge of the essence, then the *truth* of factual knowledge, i.e., correctness, for its part must also be grounded in the truth of the knowledge of the essence. Truth as correctness (ὁμοίωσις) has its ground in truth as unconcealedness (ἀλήθεια), the coming-forth, and being in view in advance, of the beingness (essence) of beings. What is seen in a productive seeing and claimed as the ground of the positing of truth as correctness is truth as ἀλήθεια. Ἀλήθεια (the unconcealedness of beings as such) is now the original and genuinely Greek name for truth, because it names the more original essence of truth. Neither the Latin word *veritas* nor our German word *Wahrheit* ["truth"] contain the least echo of what the Greeks saw in advance and experienced when they spoke about truth in their sense: ἀλήθεια.

§26. *Unconcealedness and the openness of beings. The process of the submergence of the original Greek essence of truth in the sense of the unconcealedness of beings.*

Where do we now stand? We asked how the ordinary definition of truth, of the essence of the true—namely, the correctness of an assertion—was founded originally in Aristotle. We showed that because the positing of correctness as the essence of truth accomplishes an essential positing, there can be no question of a foundation, which is the reason we seek in vain for one. Nevertheless, the positing of the essence is not arbitrary but is the positing of a ground, the taking up of that which makes possible what is to be grasped in its essence and gives it its ground.

What then provides the ground for truth conceived as correctness? The ground of correctness (ὁμοίωσις) is ἀλήθεια, the unconcealedness of beings. What does ἀ-λήθεια, the unconcealedness of beings, mean? Nothing else but that beings as such are not concealed and not closed, and hence are open. The *openness* of beings proves to be the ground of the possibility of correctness. And that is exactly what we brought out at the beginning of our inquiry. We showed that the openness of beings lies at the ground of the ordinary conception of truth as correctness, and we saw the need to question this openness as such in order to grasp the essence of truth originally. We contended that this openness is what is properly worthy of questioning in the question of truth. And we saw that the Greeks already knew this openness of beings; indeed, they took ἀλήθεια, the unconcealedness of beings, as the proper essence of truth. Furthermore, for the Greeks the true is in advance the unconcealed, and truth is the same as the unconcealedness of beings. Only because of such a productive seeing of truth on the part of the Greeks could the possibility of the assimilation to beings of a proposition or representation not be a question for them and not at all be in need of a foundation; on the contrary, with regard to ἀλήθεια such an assimilation presents itself as self-evident. Were the Greeks thus aware that the correctness of an assertion requires the openness of beings as its essential ground? If so, *our* referring to what is worthy of questioning in the ordinary conception of truth is wholly superfluous and exceedingly belated. There is no longer anything to ask here because the Greeks have already answered the question of truth.

Thus if we today want to rise above the ordinary conception of truth as correctness, and if we must do so to grasp it in its proper essence and ground, and in that way answer the question of truth sufficiently, then there is obviously no need at all for toil on our part; we simply have to return to what Greek philosophy has already seen. At most, we would need to recall something forgotten. Nor is this forgetting itself very remarkable, because from the time of Aristotle, or even since Plato, the conception of truth as the correctness of an assertion has been the standard, and the only standard, for the determination of the essence of truth, and the name ἀλήθεια was then employed spontaneously to express the correctness of an assertion, i.e., to name this standard determination of the essence of truth as correctness. And when in the process of recasting the Greek way of speaking, i.e., in the transformation of the Greek way of thinking and basic attitude toward beings into the Roman and later Western modes, ἀλήθεια was translated as *veritas*, then not only was the established conception of truth as correctness transmitted, but, at the same time, through the translation of ἀλήθεια as *veritas* every resonance of the original essence of truth as ἀλήθεια, unconcealedness, was destroyed. This resonance is also completely suppressed by our word "truth." Ἀλήθεια henceforth means, according to the essential determination of truth, the same as the correctness of an assertion. What the Greeks once saw and experienced as the original essence of truth no longer has any effect; it has been submerged. (*Verum nominat id in quod tendit intellectus. . . . Veritas principaliter est in intellectu.*)[1]

This process had a still further consequence: to the extent that later centuries up to the most recent times recalled the philosophy of the Greeks and took pains to present their doctrine of truth, truth was then of course grasped in the sense of *veritas*, as the correctness of an assertion of judging reason. This later determination of the essence of ἀλήθεια as the only valid one was then sought within Greek philosophy, even where a conception of truth as correctness was foreign, i.e., where the original experience of truth as unconcealedness still prevailed. This led to the ludicrous contention that the early Greek thinkers were dabblers and incapable of clearly conceiving the essence of truth and the "problem" of knowledge and judgment, and that only Plato and Aristotle succeeded in doing so.

Thus everything was stood on its head. And this inversion still rules the ordinary scholarly presentation of Greek philosophy. But still more essential than this inverted scholarship itself is the fact that it has blocked our access to the original essence of truth. How so? From what we have said, do we not merely need to get used to translating the Greek word ἀλήθεια with our word "unconcealedness" instead of "truth" in the sense of cor-

1. Thomas Aquinas, *Summa Theologica*, vol. I, question XVI, article 1. In *Opera Omnia*, Parma, 1852. ["The true names that towards which the intellect tends . . . Truth is principally in the intellect"—Tr.]

rectness? People have said benignly that the merit of the treatise *Being and Time* was to have brought back into circulation this literal translation of ἀλήθεια. Ἀλήθεια is now translated as "unconcealedness," and—everything remains as it was. For nothing is gained by a mere change in the way of speaking, not even if, beyond the literal translation of ἀλήθεια, it is shown that the Greeks already knew the unconcealedness of beings to be the essence of truth.

Such an improvement in the historiographical presentation of the Greek conception of truth is far removed from a historical reflection on the question of truth—so far removed that the improvement in the way of speaking actually further impedes this reflection and its necessity. For it is now well known that the Greeks had already appealed to the openness of beings as truth. But modern and contemporary philosophy also know, more than anything else, that, in the progress of philosophical thinking, Plato and Aristotle overcame this early Greek conception of truth. In the course of modern thought, the doctrine that truth is the correctness of the judging reason (*intellectus*) developed into such a matter of course that even the greatest antagonist of this thinking, Nietzsche, does not tamper with the doctrine in the least but instead makes it the foundation of his own theory of truth. In doing so, Nietzsche is unwittingly in perfect agreement with Thomas Aquinas, who said, on the basis of a particular interpretation of Aristotle: *veritas* principaliter *est in intellectu*: truth has its place, above all and originally, in judging reason. Every connection with the early Greek conception of truth—truth as the unconcealedness of beings—is therefore stigmatized as a relapse into a standpoint that has been overcome long ago and was valid only for the rudimentary beginnings of Western thought.

What has now been accomplished? Where have we arrived since we deflected from our simply stated course of questioning onto an apparent side track? We questioned back from the ordinary conception of truth (truth as the correctness of an assertion) into what we called openness—which we introduced as being genuinely worthy of questioning. Openness, however, can constitute the more original essence of truth only if that of which it is the ground, namely correctness, for its part touches upon the essence of truth in some way, even if not originally. Does it touch the essence—i.e., is the usual conception of truth founded, and if so, how? We have seen that this conception and determination of the essence of truth is in fact *not* founded, because, as a positing of essence, it cannot be founded in the usual sense at all. Yet it is not therefore without ground; on the contrary, what is claimed as the ground of the possibility of correctness is ἀλήθεια, and that is for the Greeks the essence of truth. The unconcealedness of beings as such is the ground of the possibility of correctness. For the Greeks, it is even in a pre-eminent sense that unconcealedness (ἀλήθεια) as the essence of truth is the ground of the possibility of correctness (ὁμοίωσις). Let us reflect: the Greeks did not begin by positing correctness as the essence of truth in order then to go back to unconcealedness as its ground; on the contrary, they first experienced the unconcealedness of beings and on the basis of this experience determined truth *also* as the correctness of an assertion, in that they—in light of ἀλήθεια—saw the possibility and the necessity of ὁμοίωσις. Hence this subsequent conception of the essence of truth as correctness, from which *we* began, is very well grounded and indeed grounded precisely in that wherein Greek thought and knowledge of beings move in advance: in the unconcealedness of beings. And thus it is grounded in the same ground to which our critical reflection was referred back, namely the openness of beings, as we called it. Consequently, the approach of our critical reflection—to begin with the ordinary conception of truth as correctness—is justified. But at the same time it turns out that this critical reflection is now superfluous, because what it discovers, the unconcealedness of beings, was already experienced by the Greeks and was taken up by them as the ground of the possibility of correctness. The openness we found worthy of questioning at the beginning of our critical reflection was already appreciated by the Greeks, so much so that this unconcealedness of beings became for them the primordial determination of the essence of truth. Consequently, the Greeks had already worked out exactly what we have been trying to take up as the more original and necessary task of future philosophical inquiry.

RECAPITULATION

1) The productive seeing of the unconcealedness of beings as the ground of the essence of truth as correctness.

Our task was to answer this question: how is the essential determination of truth as correctness founded? Since there is no foundation for the positing of an essence, the positing of the essence being in itself the laying of a ground, we had to pose the question of foundation in another way. So we asked what is seen and brought forth as the ground of that essence of truth? What is taken up as that in which truth in the sense of correctness is rooted and out of which it, so to say, blossoms forth? What is the reference back, what is the source, what is seen in advance in the case of the positing of the essence of truth as correctness? The truth whose essence is *subsequently* determined as correctness was called by the Greeks, prior to this determination, ἀλήθεια, unconcealedness. And what they meant was the unconcealedness of beings themselves—the unconcealedness of beings as such. Originally, there resides in this determination of truth as unconcealedness nothing like correctness, but, instead, all correctness of assertions resides in the unconcealedness of beings. For the orientation of representations toward beings and their conformity with beings are possible only if beings dwell in unconcealedness. Consequently, if the correctness of representing and asserting is posited for what it is, then along with it ἀλήθεια, the unconcealedness of beings, must also be posited and be in view as what provides this essence its ground. In positing the essence of truth as the correctness of an assertion, the Greeks already had in view, they saw in advance and brought forth, the ground of this positing, i.e., ἀλήθεια. In different terms, the delimitation of truth as correctness is a limiting conception developed in only one determined respect and hence is a limited grasp of the foundational truth as the unconcealedness of beings.

2) The Greek ἀλήθεια as openness. The transformation of the concept of truth from unconcealedness to correctness.

Where do we then stand? At the start of our inquiry—taking our departure from the ordinary concept of truth (correctness of an assertion)—we carried out a critical reflection that pointed back to a more original essence of truth, which we called openness. But the source of this critique, namely, that to which something more original is assigned, was itself not immediately justified. The reflection on justification, accomplished along with the first positing of the essence of truth as correctness, showed, however, that this justification of the positing of the essence derives its right from the unconcealedness of beings, consequently precisely from that toward which our critical reflection on the ordinary concept of truth led back. What else is the ἀλήθεια of the Greeks but what we call openness? Therefore what is needed first is not at all a laborious critique of the traditional concept of truth. What is required is simply that we remember its historical origin and its primordial justification, hence, that we call back something forgotten.

The forgetting of the ground of the traditional concept of truth, hence the forgetting of its original essence, which was once revealed, is easily explained. By the transformation of Greek thinking into Roman, Christian, and modern concepts, ἀλήθεια as ὁμοίωσις, correctness, became *veritas* as *adaequatio* and *rectitudo*, i.e., truth as adequation and correctness. What was lost was not only every resonance of the meaning of ἀλήθεια, the Greek name for *veritas* and truth, but, above all, every impulse to gain some sort of knowledge of the position of Greek humanity within beings and toward beings, out of which alone such essential words as ἀλήθεια could be spoken. Instead, due to the misunderstanding of its essence, ἀλήθεια was understood everywhere as the correctness of a representation.

At the same time we must note well that in the history of Western philosophy since the Greeks, not only did this forgetting of their primordial concept of truth come to pass, but more happened: on the basis of this transformed concept of truth—in the sense of the correctness of an assertion or a representation—new basic philosophical positions arose with Descartes and Leibniz, with Kant and the thinkers of German idealism, and lastly with Nietzsche. All this occurred, to be sure, within a unanimity of thinking and in a uniformity of the guiding lines of inquiry, so that, e.g., in spite of the abysmal differences between the medieval theologian Thomas Aquinas and the last essential thinker of the West, Nietzsche, for both of them the same conception of truth, as a characteristic of judging reason, was authoritative. And this did not at all occur on the basis of an explicit reflection but entirely as if it were all beyond question—where indeed it still stands today.

The result of everything here is that our critical reflection is superfluous, because it has already been accomplished. Furthermore, this accomplishment has long since been overcome. Therefore our presumably more original question into the essence of truth is without necessity. In fact, everything comes down to this: Does our inquiry arise merely from an unfounded resistance against the past, hence in the end from a blind and simple desire for novelty—or from a necessity? And if so, from which one?

At this point we see at once that it is not possible in philosophy—as it is in science—for a critical question to demonstrate itself on the basis of an objective state of affairs. The philosophical question must bear its necessity within itself; it must—if sufficiently unfolded—make this necessity itself visible. Therefore, if now, after this first substantive clarification of the domain of the inquiry, we reflect on the necessity of the question, we are not thereby abandoning the question of truth, and are not leaving it behind, but are performing the very first step leading to its unfolding.

Chapter Four

The Necessity of the Question of the Essence of Truth, on the Basis of the Beginning of the History of Truth

§27. *The turning of the critical question of truth toward the beginning of the history of truth as a leaping ahead into the future.* Ἀλήθεια *as experienced by the Greeks though not interrogated by them.*

First of all, do our previous discussions of the question of truth contribute toward exhibiting the necessity of that question? To be sure. Thus the elucidation of the Greek concept of truth was in no way superfluous.

1. It showed that the Greeks were already acquainted with two senses of truth: first as unconcealedness (openness of beings) and then as the assimilation of a representation to beings (correctness).

2. This observation protects us from the preposterous claim of having raised a "new" question with our initial critique of the ordinary concept of truth. If a recognition of the greatness of Greek thinking keeps us, at the very outset, free from such preposterous notions and from the desire for novelty, our discussion of the Greek notion of truth will then have a special significance for our inquiry, and everything comes down to this:

3. Our critical questioning back from the ordinary concept of truth as the correctness of an assertion to the openness of beings

is not an arbitrary critique, stemming from empty hair-splitting, but is the turning of our thinking and questioning about truth toward the beginning of the history of truth. And we today still dwell in this history, indeed precisely insofar as we unwittingly and as a matter of course in all our thinking and acting move within the domain of the traditional concept of truth.

Just what have we gained thereby? What else than the historiographical cognition that for us today, and for the West since long ago, the original essence of truth has been lost because of the predominance of truth as correctness. Hence we have gained the recognition of a loss. But it is not at all decided that we have here a genuine loss. For that would be the case only if it could be shown that the not-losing, the preservation, of the original essence of truth (ἀλήθεια) is a necessity and that we consequently need to gain back what was lost.

Yet, even assuming this were demonstrated conclusively, *can* we gain back what was lost? Is the past not irreparably gone? And even if we wanted to adhere to this past in memory, would that not lead to the opposite of what is necessary? We do not want to turn back history, and of course we cannot; instead, we must think and act out of our present (or future) necessity. For the shocks (world war, world revolution) or, rather, that of which these shocks are merely the historical consequences have forced us—not any single individuals, nor the still more arbitrary "many," and not individual peoples or nations and states for themselves, but the entire West—into the question of whether or not we are still in the truth, indeed whether we still want and can want the truth at all.

In view of this task, is not the merely retrospective remembering of earlier times—no matter how essential these times may have been—yet still "historicism," an adherence to the past from some sort of ill-concealed "romanticism" or from some "humanistic" predilection, now basically antiquated, for the Greeks and the Greek world and its philosophy? Or does the retrospection originate merely in an antipathy toward the degeneration of what today, under the venerable name of philosophy, postures in an unbridled and uninhibited writing of books and blabbering, the extent and content of which stand in a reverse relation to the power to raise essential questions? But can we be permitted to base our entire approach and procedure on mere antipathies? Is this revival of Greek thinking not basically a flight from the necessities pressing hard upon us, a blindness in relation to the present, and a shrinking back before the future? Is this not always the case with such reversions to the early and the earliest and the "beginning"; do they not show that one's own power has flagged and all possibilities have been exhausted?

Our discussions of the Greek concept of truth and the insight they provided, namely that our critical questioning is a turning back toward primordial Greek thought, might be more than free-floating historiographical considerations. They might contain something of a historical reflection, for they bring before the inner eye the distance between the present and the past. Nevertheless, we cannot rid ourselves of the suspicion that in all this, instead of assuming the tasks of today, we are undertaking a more or less well disguised scholarly stroll into the harmless past, providing us with mere historiographical cognitions instead of indicating what we ourselves should do to throw off all the early things of the beginning and leave them behind.

But against all these obvious, and largely justified, objections we must reflect on what we said, perhaps only conjecturally, about the beginning of the history of Western thought: the beginning could be something which, furled in its greatness, reaches ahead into the future, and, accordingly, the return to the beginning could be a leaping ahead, indeed a genuine leaping ahead into the future, though to be sure only under the condition that we really do begin with the beginning.

That is now the decisive question, *the* question, whose answer decides the necessity or arbitrariness of our procedure and consequently decides the question of truth as such. The preceding discussion of the history of the Greek notion of truth took us back temporally more than two millennia, yet we have perhaps not at all arrived at the beginning of this history—not because our question has not gone back far enough in time but because in this way we are not yet within history at all and again and again fall back into historiographical considerations, reckoning the present against the past, instead of actually reflecting.

We have made the historiographical constatation that the Greeks, at the beginning of their thinking, conceived of truth as ἀλήθεια, as the unconcealedness of beings, and only very much later, specifically at the end of their great philosophy—in the thought of Plato and in the doctrines of Aristotle—passed on to a determination of truth as the correctness of an assertion. With this positing of the essence they then took up the earlier and more original conception of truth as the "natural" ground of truth in the sense of correctness. This historiographical constatation is indisputable. But it is by no means a historical reflection, which—as we know—only springs forth out of genuine questioning on the part of the one who is reflecting and must also remain supported by it. Hence we have to ask first of all:

When the Greeks took up ἀλήθεια (unconcealedness) as the ground of correctness, did they thereby posit this ground as ground and did they ground it as such? Furthermore, assuming they grounded the unconcealedness of beings as the ground of correctness, is this ground itself— ἀλήθεια in *its* essence—thereby sufficiently determined and questioned? Did the Greeks ever interrogate ἀλήθεια as such; did they deem the unconcealedness of beings as such worthy of questioning? The Greeks experienced the essence of truth as unconcealedness—does that mean without further ado that for them this very unconcealedness was worthy of questioning? By no means. The Greeks once experienced the unconcealedness of beings and took it up as truth, and on this ground they determined truth as correctness and posited this ground and grounded it, but they did not go further and explicitly interrogate unconcealedness itself. Ἀλήθεια remained for them unquestioned. Their thinking did not penetrate further into ἀλήθεια as such, and they did not fathom [*er-gründet*] it explicitly in its essence. Instead, they merely stood under the force of the emerging but still furled essence of truth as unconcealedness.

§28. *Truth as correctness and its domination over its own ground as an essential consequence of the absence of a fathoming of the ground. The question of openness as the question of* ἀλήθεια *itself.*

The positing of something as the ground for something else, the grounding of the ground, is not yet *genuine* grounding in the sense of a fathoming of the ground. What then are we to make of this occurrence, namely that the Greeks experienced ἀλήθεια precisely as the essence of truth and took it up as the ground of correctness but did not themselves explicitly fathom this ground? What if the effect was that henceforth truth as correctness acquired domination over that in which it is rooted? What if this occurrence, that the thinking of the Greeks did not master ἀλήθεια, led to the situation that this beginning was submerged in the following times and remains submerged even today? And what if this occurrence were thereby not something bygone but would now still be coming to pass insofar as we move in the ungrounded obviousness of the traditional concept of truth?

And in fact that is what is happening. The knowledge of the essence of ἀλήθεια did not get lost *because* later on ἀλήθεια was translated by *veritas*, *rectitudo*, and "truth," and was interpreted as the correctness of an assertion, but just the opposite, this translation and this new interpretation could begin and could gain prevalence only because the essence of ἀλήθεια was not unfolded originally enough and its unfolding was not grounded strongly enough. The occurrence of the submergence of the primordial essence of truth, unconcealedness (ἀλήθεια), is nothing past and gone but is immediately present and operative in the basic fact it determines, namely the unshaken domination of the traditional concept of truth.

Within the realm of the history of what is essential, only rarely does something occur. What does occur there happens very slowly and very silently, and its immediate effect leaps over the span of millennia. It does not need the crutches of a continuous chain of cause and effect, each effect becoming the cause of a succeeding one. If historiographers were required to assume the task of presenting what is essential, they would flounder in the greatest embarrassment, not because they have too much at their disposal but too little. What would remain of the whole business of archives and literature, what would remain of the business of reviews and dissertations, if by one stroke what is unessential became ungraspable? But that will not happen, for the unessential, in very different forms, is the long shadow cast by the essential, to end up mostly overshadowed by it. The occurrence of the submergence of primordial ἀλήθεια exists still, and it occurs wherever truth means correctness.

Only if we submit to this knowledge will we be on the path of historical reflection. Only in that way will we arrive historically—rather than historiographically—back at the beginning of Western reflection on truth, back at what occurred primordially and is still occurring. Only through such reflection will we put ourselves in a position to begin with the beginning, and that means to be *futural* in an original way instead of merely reckoning back historiographically to the earliest past and exposing its difference, or indeed backwardness, in comparison with the present.

Consequently our question about the ground of the possibility of correctness, hence the return to openness and above all the question of openness itself as the most worthy of questioning, is not superfluous. It is so little superfluous that this interrogation actually becomes the making good of an earlier neglect, the making good of the question of what ἀλήθεια itself is, the question the Greeks never raised.

Now we emphasize anew that the beginning is the greatest, surpassing everything that comes afterward, even if this turns against the beginning, which it can do only because the beginning *is* and makes possible what succeeds it. So is it not pure pedantry when we say the Greeks have neglected a question here? Is it not a very arrogant underestimation of the greatness of their thinking to say they did not master the question of truth? To be sure, it is. Thus even our attempted reflection on the primordial Greek thinking about the essence of truth is not yet sufficiently reflective, i.e., it will not attain the beginning historically enough, so long as this reflection terminates in the presumptuous superiority of the epigones over the founding masters. As long as it does so, we are not yet in the proper position to begin with the beginning, i.e., to be futural, to seize and prepare our future in thought and questioning.

We must therefore reflect on this occurrence, that the Greeks did indeed experience the essence of truth as unconcealedness, took it up, and always had it available to them, but did not question it explicitly and did not fathom it. Was this event mere neglect and the result of an incapacity of questioning, or does the genuine greatness of Greek thought consist precisely in this and accomplish itself in it? The decision here is not an attempt to explain and rescue a past incident—the Greek thinkers do not need that—but is instead the delimitation of the way *we* take a stand toward truth and stand in the truth. For what came to pass at the beginning of the history of the essential foundation of truth always remains for us still to be decided—a decision about what for us and for the future can become true and can be true.

The Greeks experienced the essence of truth originally as ἀλήθεια, as the unconcealedness of beings. This essence of truth, however, was not first captured in a "definition" and made available to knowledge. Definitions in philosophy—though not in science—always come late and usually come last. The knowledge of the essence of truth as the unconcealedness of beings had originally, i.e., in its great epoch, this form, that all acting and creating, all thinking and speaking, all founding and proceeding were determined by and thoroughly in accord with the unconcealedness of beings as something ungrasped. Whoever does not see and does not know this, and cannot learn to see and know it, will never divine anything of the original event of the beginning of Western history, of that beginning which really was its beginning, inasmuch as we mean the *history* of the West and not the mere biology of its peoples—about which we do not know anything anyway, not only because the sources are meager, but because the presupposition for interpreting it, our knowledge of "life," is so miserable and confused.

That the Greeks were primordial in thought and poetry and politics is evident most starkly in the fact that the end in which we find ourselves today is nothing else than a decline from their beginning, an increasing inability to be equal to the beginning. Yet this does not exclude our own creating and working in the aftermath and tradition of this beginning. To be equal to requires a surpassing. But how can we expect such a thing when we can barely achieve the most wretched imitations? One might think here of the massive classical movement in art, which arose out of the void and gapes into the void. The surpassing of the beginning occurs only within another beginning, one which recognizes that its surpassing merely surpasses the aftermath and the tradition of the beginning and can "only" reach the level of the beginning, for nothing higher can be attained.

§29. *The Greeks' experience of unconcealedness as the basic character of beings as such and their lack of inquiry into* ἀλήθεια.

How are we to understand truth in the sense of the unconcealedness of beings so that it might allow us to see why the Greeks did not explicitly interrogate unconcealedness, allow us to know how to judge this lack of inquiry, and allow us to experience thereby the necessities we ourselves are drawn into?

The experience of truth as the unconcealedness of beings implies first of all that truth is—to say it quite indeterminately—a character of beings themselves, and not, as in the ordinary view of later times, a matter of assertions about beings. For the Greeks, but only for them, beings themselves are what can be true or untrue, i.e., unconcealed or dissembled.

To obviate misunderstandings in this regard, a short excursus is needed. In the following times, every being, *ens*, was indeed still conceived as *verum*, and scholasticism as well as a part of modern philosophy spoke of "ontological" truth in distinction to the "logical" truth of the intellect. Now this doctrine does in fact stem from a particular adherence to the tradition of Greek philosophy, but it is thought and intended wholly and utterly in an un-Greek way. *Verum* does not mean the unconcealed; on the contrary, *omne ens est verum*—"Every being is true"—because, as a being, it is in advance necessarily thought of *correctly* by God or, according to Christian and Old Testament thinking, by the "creator," i.e., by the creator as the absolute spirit free from error. We note this parenthetically in order to avert the commingling and identification, attempted again and again, of Thomistic thinking with Aristotelian thought and Greek thinking in general. This identification is often advanced not only by representatives of Thomism but even by classical philologists. For example, the theory Werner Jaeger has disseminated about Aristotle is much more medieval and scholastic than Greek. Both medieval and modern thinking move wholly within a conception of truth as correctness, i.e., as a determination of knowledge—even when they speak of "ontological truth." This "ontological" truth is nothing else than the correlate of God's thinking, which is in itself absolutely correct. It is not the unconcealed in the Greek sense but is the absolutely *correct* (*intellectus divinus*). A still deeper foundation for this is the evidence that all traditional ontology determines the *ens qua ens* under the guidance of the act of thinking and *its* truth, i.e., correctness.

If the Greeks experienced truth as a characteristic of beings, then this truth must be founded in beings themselves. Or should we not rather say here that the truth as a characteristic of beings belongs to these beings? Should the truth as experienced by the Greeks characterize the essence of beings themselves, i.e., of beings themselves as understood by the Greeks? These are not questions posed to empty possibilities; they are well warranted, for precisely where another conception of truth (as the correctness of an assertion) had already developed and established itself in Greek philosophy, namely in Plato and Aristotle, beings and truth were always mentioned together: ἀλήθεια καὶ ὄν—"unconcealedness: *that is to say*, beings as such."[1] Beyond a doubt, we are to understand καὶ here as an explication, in the sense of "and that is to say," for often instead of even mentioning ὄν, they said simply ἀλήθεια or τὸ ἀληθές.

It goes so much against our habits to think of unconcealedness, with complete decisiveness, as characteristic of beings as such that even when we have gained insight into the distinction between the unconcealedness of beings and the correctness of an assertion, we still too readily conceive of unconcealedness as detached from beings, as if it were an addition, accessory to beings.

But why did the Greeks not inquire into ἀλήθεια as such, if it does indeed belong to beings themselves, and if in fact the question of beings as such was the primordial and constant question of the Greek thinkers? Why did ἀλήθεια remain precisely the unquestioned? Why did it not become the most worthy of questioning? And when ἀλήθεια was interrogated explicitly, why did the very way of questioning turn ἀλήθεια as unconcealedness into ἀλήθεια as correctness? We today are hardly able to measure the full consequences of this determination and are likely to take them, in spite of everything, as historiographical subtleties relating to what is long past and gone, rather than as directives to a decisive event which is still decisive over us; nevertheless, we must put this questioning aside now and attempt a first answer.

1. Cf. Plato, *Republic* VI.

Why did the Greeks not make ἀλήθεια as such a question, rather than—if we may say so—experience it as something "obvious"? Was this lack of inquiry a neglect? Did it stem from impotence with regard to original questioning?

RECAPITULATION

1) The ground of the necessity of the question of the essence of truth.

Even without special reflection, the question of truth seems important enough. But although we might take an emphatic interest in "truth," i.e., in what is true and in the possession of what is true, that still does not qualify as a sufficient ground for the *necessity* of the question of the *essence* of truth. For the history of the essence of truth and the still unbroken obviousness of the traditional conception of truth testify quite clearly that the necessity of this question about the essence has by no means been experienced and seen with insight. Now the necessity of a philosophical question is as essential as the question itself is. For a philosophical question must, following the sovereign character of philosophy, bear in itself its necessity, i.e., it must point back to this necessity. Therefore we could not have begun with a reflection on the necessity of the question of truth, but instead the first task had to be to develop this question according to its initially graspable basic features, in order for this development itself to lead us to the necessity of the question.

Hereby a view is opened up on the essence of philosophy which we cannot further investigate now, but which must be briefly noted, since it clarifies the ground of the appurtenance of historical reflection to meditative questioning. The domain of philosophy as the question of beings as such and as a whole, and consequently philosophy itself, cannot be manufactured and determined by human products and institutions and claims. The human output and "work" to be found under the name "philosophy," in any of its forms, will never make visible what philosophy is. For philosophy belongs to the truth of Being. Philosophy *is* and *must be* whenever and however Being itself presses toward its truth, i.e., when the openness of beings themselves comes to pass, when history *is*. Philosophy, if it is, does not exist because there are philosophers, nor are there philosophers because philosophy is taken up. On the contrary, philosophy and philosophers exist only when and how the truth of Being itself comes to pass, a history which is withdrawn from every human institution and plan, since it itself is the very ground for the possibility of human historical Being. This may serve to indicate the direction out of which we must experience the necessity of the question of the essence of truth, assuming we are able to and want to experience it.

2) Ἀλήθεια as primordial for the Greeks yet unquestioned by them.

The preceding path of our reflections gave rise to the insight that that toward which our critical deliberation had to question back, namely the openness of beings as the ground of the possibility of the correctness of an assertion, was already known in Greek thinking as ἀλήθεια, the unconcealedness of beings. Consequently, our critical reflections, and thereby the question of truth itself, have no original necessity. They are superfluous, because they only bring back something already accomplished. Our critical reflection may indeed signify a turning in the direction of the thinking of Greek philosophy, but thereby it shows itself—in addition to being superfluous—as a flight into the past, no matter how highly prized.

But as certain as it is that what we are calling the openness of beings is connected to what the Greeks called ἀλήθεια, that is how undecided it is whether our question, its *what* and its *how*, was also a question raised by the Greeks. That alone matters here. Now it has been shown that the Greeks did indeed primordially take up ἀλήθεια in the sense of the unconcealedness of beings as the essence of truth and founded upon it the determination of ἀλήθεια as ὁμοίωσις but that they precisely did not ask about ἀλήθεια itself and its essence. Furthermore, because they did not raise this question of the essence of ἀλήθεια, of unconcealedness as such, because for the Greeks ἀλήθεια remained primordial and unquestioned, therefore the determination of truth as correctness, which was actually grounded upon it, could gain an ascendancy over ἀλήθεια, could thrust it aside, and could by itself dominate the subsequent history of thought.

So if in fact the Greeks did not raise the question we are raising in making the openness of beings what is most worthy of questioning, then we are facing an omission and a neglect, especially in view of the incontrovertible passion of the Greeks to give a reason and an accounting for what they thought: λόγον διδόναι. On the other hand, however, we find it difficult to indulge in the self-righteous pedantry of accusing the primordial thinking of the Greeks, which, as the beginning, was the greatest, of such a lack.

The question therefore is why the Greeks did not ask about ἀλήθεια itself. Is their lack of inquiry a neglect? In order to reach an answer here we have to determine more closely the Greeks' primordial conception of ἀλήθεια. We translate ἀλήθεια as the unconcealedness *of beings* and thereby already indicate that unconcealedness (truth as understood by the Greeks) is a determination of beings themselves and not—as is correctness—a character of assertions *about* beings.

Yet the modes of thinking and speaking in Greek philosophy compel us still further. Plato and Aristotle, precisely the two thinkers who prepared the submergence of the primordial essence of ἀλήθεια, still always mentioned ἀλήθεια together with beings themselves: ἀλήθεια καὶ ὄν—"unconcealedness: that is to say, beings in their beingness." Often ἀλήθεια even stood alone in place of ὄν. Truth and beings in their beingness are the same. The result of all this is not simply that unconcealedness is related to beings themselves instead of to assertions about beings, but that unconcealedness constitutes the basic character of beings themselves as such.

How are we to understand that? Above all, how are we then to understand that the Greeks precisely did not ask about ἀλήθεια? For the most primordially proper question of their thought, guiding all their reflection, was precisely the question of beings as such: what is a being? Ἀλήθεια itself is a character of beings. It lay before the Greeks, as it were, in the immediate direction of the questioning that was most their own. Consequently, if ἀλήθεια indeed resided in the direction of their questioning, was their failure to question it not a neglect? In other words, did the thinking power of the Greeks fall short here?

§30. *Their fidelity to the destiny meted out to them as the reason the Greeks did not ask about* ἀλήθεια. *Non-occurrence as what is necessarily detained in and through the beginning.*

No. The reason the Greeks did not inquire here is that this question runs counter to their ownmost task, and therefore it could not at all enter their field of view. Their failure to question was not a consequence of a lack of power but was due precisely to their original power to remain faithful to the destiny meted out to them.

What was the task assigned them? How can we tell? We are not capable of calculating it. If we try to, we end up merely with a list of their opinions, we end up with a report on the views they held. For the curious, for those who love to know a thinker's "standpoint," the "views" of a philosopher are indeed all that is desired; for a philosophy, however, this is completely a matter of indifference. The task assigned to the primordial thinkers is accessible only through a reflection on their primordial questioning. The past counts for nothing, the beginning for everything. Hence our ever more penetrating inquiry back into the beginning. Hence even our reflection concerning the ground for what did *not* occur at the beginning. For what did not happen in history in the essential moments of history—and what would be more essential than a beginning?—must still come to pass, not as a mere repetition but in the sense of those jolts, leaps, and bounds, in the sense of that momentary and simple, which we must concentrate upon and be prepared for, if we are really to expect of future history something essential.

In the realm of what is essential, what does not occur is even more essential than what does, for it can never become a matter of indifference but instead always stands, and ever more firmly, within the possibility of becoming more necessary and more compelling. On the other hand, the occurrence of the essential is almost inevitably followed by its being covered over and submerged by the unessential. As is clear, then, the non-occurrence we are speaking of is by no means just any arbitrary thought, detached from all necessity. On the contrary, the non-occurrence here is something necessarily held back and detained in the beginning and through the beginning, whereby the beginning remains the unfathomable, which ever anew instigates reflection on itself—with more difficulty, the further the decline has progressed.

§31. *The end of the first beginning and the preparation for another beginning.*

a) Our situation at the end of the beginning and the demand for a reflection on the first beginning as a preparation for another beginning.

We need to reflect here on the beginning of Western thinking and on what occurred in it and did not occur in it, because we stand at the end—at the end of this beginning. That is, we are standing before the decision between the end (and its running out, which may still take centuries) and another beginning, one which can only be a moment, but whose preparation requires the patience "optimists" are no more capable of than "pessimists."

Yet it might be said that here—as elsewhere—there is no need for a special decision between end and beginning, since nobody wants the end right away, and everyone altogether prefers the beginning and its continuation. But this decision is not made in the well-tended garden of our inclinations, wishes, and intentions. If the decision is set there, it is no decision. It takes place in the domain of our preparedness or unpreparedness for the future. This domain is opened up—*if* it does indeed unfurl—according to the originality enabling us to find ourselves again in what genuinely occurs, out of lostness in our contrivances and endeavors, out of entanglement in what is obvious and worn out. But we will find ourselves there only through a reflection on the beginning and on what was entrusted to it. For we are thoroughly successors to and heirs of a long history, and we are satisfied by and avid for historiographical cognition and its account of the past. Historiography is a narcotic averting us from history. Even if we simply want to prepare the other beginning, we will achieve that only if we are mobilized for the extraordinary and for what is perhaps still reserved and held open for us, namely the possibility of beginning with the beginning, i.e., with the first beginning, while bringing it beyond itself into its future—out of *another* beginning.

We must reflect on the first beginning of Western thought because we stand at its end. Our use of the word "end" is ambiguous here. On the one hand, it means we stand in the domain of that end which is the end *of* the first beginning. In this sense, end does not mean either the mere cessation or the waning of the power of the beginning. On the contrary, the end of a real and essential history can itself only be an essential one. It is in this sense of "end" that we have to understand Nietzsche's philosophy and its astonishingly unique greatness and form—a philosophy whose essential influence has not yet even begun. The greatness of the end consists not only in the essentiality of the closure of the great possibilities but also in the power to prepare a transition to something wholly other.

At the same time, however, "end" refers to the running out and the dissipation of all the effects of the previous history of Western thinking. That is, it refers to a confusion of the traditional basic positions, value concepts, and propositions in the usual interpretation of beings, a confusion that will presumably smolder for a long time still and is already unrecognizable as such. We are standing at the end in this double sense. Therefore we must reflect on the beginning.

b) The experience of the end by Hölderlin and Nietzsche and their reflection on the beginning of Western history.

Despite this brief clarification, the demand just articulated concerning a reflection on the beginning would be entirely arbitrary and presumptuous if we did not know—or, more prudently, if we could not know—that Hölderlin and Nietzsche, the two who had the deepest experience of the end of the West in the double sense (not as "decline"), could endure this experience and could transform it in their creative work only through their concomitant reflection on the beginning of Western history, on what for the Greeks was necessity. If Hölderlin and Nietzsche did not stand—admittedly in a way still wholly unmastered and misunderstood—in the course of our history, then we would have no right to the demand to begin with the beginning.

That these two knew the Greek beginning, in a more original way than all previous ages, has its ground uniquely in the fact that they experienced for the first time the end of the West. To put it more sharply, they themselves, in their existence and work, became the end, each of them in a different way. Conversely, it also holds that they experienced the end and became the end only because the beginning overawed them and elevated them into greatness. Both the reflection on the first beginning and the founding of its end, an end equal to it and to its greatness, belong together in the *turning*.

The fact that both Hölderlin and Nietzsche have now become so fashionable is surely no proof that we understand what it signifies that they stand in our history as the end of its first beginning and therefore reach beyond us. On the contrary, all indications, especially the ever growing number of books and dissertations about them, testify that we are now on the verge of accounting for Hölderlin and Nietzsche historiographically and are thereby making each of them historically a dead letter.

To mention only the ill treatment of Hölderlin—mostly well-meant, as is everything we do—either his work is thought to be on behalf of the "fatherland," and excerpts are made of those passages where the words "people," "hero," and the like occur, or he is openly or surreptitiously transposed into a "Christian" and then becomes a component of a quite dubious "apologetics." Or else he is extolled as the mediator between Classicism and Romanticism. In each case, we somehow catalog the poet as just another composer of poems, dramas, and novels, next to authors such as Klopstock, Herder, Goethe, Schiller, and Kleist, instead of letting him be the decision he is, a decision whose fruitfulness literary philistines will never surmise—in the first place because they do not want to be touched by it! It is a decision over the final flight or new advent of the gods, a decision which, like every one, includes a pre-decision over our preparedness or unpreparedness with regard to such decisions.

What is the purpose of this reference to Hölderlin and Nietzsche? It is only meant to drive in this one point, that with regard to our demand to begin with the beginning even Hölderlin and Nietzsche do not provide any justification or assistance as long as we take them historiographically, even if we do so according to such high measures as "fatherland" and "Christianity." Even Hölderlin and Nietzsche, i.e., their work, must first become for us *history*, so that we might experience historically their historical reproduction of the beginning. Once again, all of this says simply that they will not be historical for us if we do not ourselves become creative in the corresponding domains or, more modestly, become preparatory and questioning. Concerning the demand to begin with the beginning, in order to overcome the end, the reference to Hölderlin and Nietzsche cannot function as an appeal to authorities but only as a directive to unmastered tasks, ones not yet even recognized, and thus only as an intimation that we are by no means dogmatically presenting a private philosophy of history.

§32. *The destiny meted out to the Greeks: to begin thinking as an inquiry into beings as such and in terms of an experience of unconcealedness as the basic character of beings (ἀλήθεια, φύσις).*

In the course of developing the question of truth, we reached the point where we had to reflect on the fact that the Greeks indeed experienced the more original essence of truth (namely, the unconcealedness of beings) but that they did not deem truth itself and its essence worthy of any original questioning, in fact so little that Greek philosophy, at the end of its golden age, even came to forsake this original essence. In view of that event, we had to ask: why did ἀλήθεια itself and as such not become for the Greeks worthy of questioning and even the most worthy of questioning? Our answer lies first of all in the form of a conjecture: it was not out of a debility in the power of thinking or even out of forgetfulness and the superficiality of always pursuing the new and the latest that the Greeks omitted the more original question of ἀλήθεια as such but out of their power to be equal to their own destiny and to carry it out all the way to its farthest extremity.

What destiny was meted out to their thought? What was the

task assigned to their thinking? Can we be so presumptuous as to dare to decide this question? For even if we simply invoke what the Greeks accomplished in matters of thinking, this accomplishment might have been a deviation from their actual destiny. Fortunately, what is at issue here is not the "results" of their philosophy but the very character of their thinking, their way of questioning, the direction from which they pursued an answer to their questioning. Their destiny was something into which they were compelled ever anew, something their thinkers, despite being basically different, nevertheless understood as the same, something that for them was therefore a necessity. Every necessity lays hold of man out of a need. Every need becomes compelling out of, and within, a basic disposition.

These directives delineate the path that might lead us to reflect on what was meted out to the Greeks as the task of thinking and might thereby lead to a reflection on the beginning.

The destiny and task of thought of the Greeks was not to think this or that but to begin thinking itself and to establish it on its ground. Thinking, as the form of the act of philosophy, here means that eruption and that procedure of man thanks to which he is established in the midst of beings, in face of beings as a whole, and knows himself as belonging to these beings. The basic work of this thinking is therefore the question of beings themselves, what they are as such and as a whole.

How did the Greeks answer this question? What sort of basic determination did they force upon beings or, better, what character of beings as such did the Greeks allow to be ascendent over themselves, so that these same Greeks might emerge and rise up in themselves?

In the context of the present lectures, we can speak about these matters only by way of certain formulas. Beings as such are φύσις. Now we must immediately put out of play all later interpretations and translations of this first, more reticent than expressive, designation of beings. That is, we must set aside all those interpretations that understand φύσις as "nature," whereby nature itself, depending on its sense in later antiquity, in Christianity, or in modernity, means quite different things, though always belonging to one single context.

Being, as such, impressed the Greeks as the constant, that

which stands in itself over and against what falls and collapses. Being—the Greeks experienced it as the constant, in the sense of the persistent, over and against the changing of what merely arises and then again disappears. The beingness of beings—that means constancy in the double sense of persistence and duration. Beings, as the constant, understood in this way in opposition to change and decay, are therefore entirely what is present, opposed to everything absent and all mere dissolution. Constancy and especially presence posit back on itself whatever comes into existence as constant and present, but they do not posit it away; they install it in itself as the uprightness of the form versus the deformity of all confusion. The constant, what is present out of itself and formed in itself, unfolds out of itself and for itself its contour and its limit, versus everything merely floating away and limitless. Constancy, presence, form, and limit—all these, especially in the simplicity of their reciprocal relations, belong to and determine what resounds in the Greek word φύσις as the designation of beings in their beingness.

Nevertheless, we have not yet mentioned the most essential determination of beings, most essential because it permeates all the other determinations. The constant, as what stands in itself and, in enduring, does not yield, stands out against decay and change and is elevated over them. What is present, as repudiating all disappearance, is what is self-representing. The form, that which holds in check all confusion, is the overwhelming and the imposing. The limit, as the defense against the limitless, suspends mere progress and rises above it. Hence, according to the determinations we mentioned, and in their mutual belonging together, a being is in the first place and entirely something that stands out against and is elevated over, something that represents itself from itself, the imposing and what has risen above—in brief: the emerging, and thus the unconcealed, over and against the concealed and the withdrawing. All determinations of the beingness of beings—the two senses of constancy, as well as presence, form, and limit—are pervaded and dominated by the one named last, the determination that genuinely should be named first: unconcealedness, ἀλήθεια.

What is the result of all this? Ἀλήθεια is for the Greeks a—indeed, *the*—basic determination of beings themselves. That will strike us today and in fact all non-Greeks as strange, and we will completely accept it only with difficulty and very slowly. Yet if we are able to repeat it, a plethora of essential insights will accompany it. Unconcealedness—that is the decisive answer to the single question of the Greek thinkers, whose questioning began the beginning of thinking, namely the question, what are beings? Ἀλήθεια as unconcealedness gathers in itself the primordial Greek meaning of the primordial word φύσις. For this word designates that which emerges from itself and unfolds itself and holds sway, such as the rose emerges and in emerging is what it is. It designates beings as such, just as a great look of the eye opens itself, and once opened and holding sway, can be found again only in a look that *perceives* it itself.

The answer to a question of thinking, and especially to *the* question of thinking, the one that first establishes all thinking in its beginning, i.e., the answer to a philosophical question, is never a result that can be detached and locked up in a proposition. Such an answer does not allow itself to be cut off from the question. On the contrary, this answer is an essential answer only if, and to the extent that, it belongs to the very questioning and is retained within it—as its completion. With regard to the usual way of thinking, intending, and questioning—and certainly altogether rightly so—the answer is that which eliminates the question. There, to answer is to satisfy and eliminate the question. But with the philosophical answer, "Beings are unconcealedness" (φύσις, ἀλήθεια), the questioning does not stop but precisely begins and unfolds itself as the beginning. That is to say, in the light of this interpretation of beings as unconcealedness, it was then the task of the Greeks to ask what beings are, to ask this more clearly, more foundationally, and more manifoldly.

RECAPITULATION

1) The lack of an inquiry into unconcealedness on the part of the Greeks and the necessity of their task.

Our inquiry into the essence of truth encountered, within a critique of the traditional concept of truth, the openness of beings.

This openness was presented as what is most questionable, as the place where the question of the essence of truth has to begin, on condition that the question of truth bears within itself a necessity proper to it, one which unfolds itself as soon as the question is raised. At the same time, it turned out that the Greeks experienced originally the essence of truth as ἀλήθεια, as the unconcealedness of beings. Openness as we intend it and unconcealedness as spoken of by the Greeks are, at least apparently, the same. There is, however, an essential distinction: for the Greeks, unconcealedness remained unquestioned; for us it is what is most worthy of questioning. Why did the Greeks not inquire into ἀλήθεια itself? Their lack of inquiry could leave us indifferent; indeed, many might rejoice that in this way some questions are still left to us. But the lack of inquiry on the part of the Greeks is not something indifferent. For we must bear in mind that to the Greeks ἀλήθεια was a—indeed *the*—determination of beings themselves and that the question of beings themselves—what they are—became *the* philosophical question of the Greeks. Thus the question of the unconcealedness of beings, and hence the question of unconcealedness itself, rested directly in the path of the most properly Greek philosophical inquiry into beings! Nevertheless, they did not raise that question. If they omitted it, not out of negligence or some other incapacity, but out of a necessity included in their very task, then we must reflect on what kind of task this was, in order to understand their lack of inquiry and thus come to know how our own questioning is related to that task.

The task of the Greeks was nothing less than the establishment of the beginning of philosophy. To understand this beginning is for us perhaps most difficult, for we are standing within the orbit of the end of that beginning.

2) Nietzsche and Hölderlin as end and as transition, each in his own way.

We understand end here in a double sense. The end, insofar as it gathers into itself all essential possibilities of the history of a beginning, is not the cessation of something over and done, but, quite to the contrary, it is an affirmation of the beginning by way of a completion of its possibilities, ones which grew out of what followed the beginning. This end of the first beginning of the history of Western philosophy is Nietzsche; in this sense and only in this sense must we interpret him in the future if his work is to be what it must also be as that end—namely, a transition. All judgment and evaluation of Nietzsche which have another orientation may very well have their determined and conditional usefulness, yet they remain philosophically inessential and erroneous. In *this* context there is no need to speak of the usual exploitation and even plundering of Nietzsche. Nietzsche is in an essential sense the end of Western philosophy.

At the same time, however, and above all, we are standing within the twilight of the end of Western thinking especially in a second sense, according to which end means the running out and the running astray of the confusion of the various basic positions, valuations, concepts, and systems as they have been prepared and formed throughout the centuries. This end—the product of an uprooted and no longer even recognizable tradition of frozen modes of thought—has its own duration, presumably one which is still to last a long time. It can yet dominate and persist, even if another beginning has begun long ago. In the protracted expiration of the end, former "modes of thought" will presumably be taken up again and again, and the end will characteristically be a succession of "renaissances."

The reception of the work of Hölderlin throughout a whole century is historical proof that the genuine end, i.e., the great echo of the greatness of the beginning, can be put aside and remain without influence.

We conclude from this that history itself is not only multi-levelled, that in it not only do successive epochs overlap, but that we know almost nothing of its genuine reality, above all because our grounds of knowledge here are insufficient and are becoming more and more insufficient due to the news media. This scarcely understood contemporary phenomenon tells us in advance what we are supposed to want to know and how we are to know it. In a transformed way, and enhanced into gigantic proportions of range and speed, the news media accomplish what was once the function of ἱστορεῖν, the exploration of remarkable things.

We of today stand—for the most part, unwittingly—to a great

extent, indeed almost exclusively, in the twilight of this expiring end of Western thinking but not yet in the orbit of the end in the first sense. For if it came to that, we would immediately proceed to a transition; but nowhere do I see in the domain of thinking, insofar as we can speak of it, a sign that a step has been taken on the great span of the bridge into the future, or indeed that such a step is even wanted.

That should not surprise us, as long as Hölderlin and Nietzsche are merely well-intentioned and familiar names and epithets. We would today hardly know anything of the character and the necessity of a reflection on the first beginning, if these both—each in a different way at once thinker and poet—did not stand in the path of our history, each, again, in a respectively different historical place. Since both of them, each in his own way, *are* end and transition, the beginning had to appear primordially to them, and a knowledge of the end had to awaken in them. Thereby Hölderlin, although further from us as reckoned historiographically, is the more futural. That is, he reaches beyond Nietzsche, not because Nietzsche himself knew Hölderlin since the end of his youth, but because Hölderlin, the poet, is further ahead than Nietzsche, the thinker, who, in spite of everything, was not able to acknowledge in an original way the primordial question of the Greeks and to unfold it. He remained precisely in this respect, more sternly than in any other, under the decisive influence of his epoch, one which was decadent in thinking and above all unrefined and lacking style.

We name and refer to Hölderlin here, as elsewhere, only within the circumference of the singular task of a thoughtful reflection on the first, and that means on the other, future, beginning of Western thinking. Hence we do not take up Hölderlin out of some sort of "aesthetic" predilection for this poet over others, i.e., out of some sort of (probably quite arbitrary) literary-historiographical evaluation of Hölderlin over and against other poets. Once again, we need to stress that our point of view on Hölderlin and the essence of poetry is unique—unique precisely in that in itself it sets itself outside of every comparison. Our intention in making visible the essence of poetry as Hölderlin has posited it in his work is not to "improve" the concept of poetry or to change it, so that a new norm might be available, with the help of which one could then also examine other poets. Such a project would at most reveal that this concept of poetry is not appropriate to other poets. Hölderlin, or his work, the latter in its entire fragmentary character, is being viewed, within the compass of our task, only as a—as *the*—not yet raised question of the future of our history, and this again only under the presupposition that the question of the essence of truth is an essential one for the preparation of this history. Thus we are here not in the least competing with the historiography of literature or the history of the spirit, and our project cannot at all be assumed therein.

Only if we hold fast to the work of Hölderlin, only if we survive the work of Nietzsche, instead of evading it, only then will our question be on its assigned path, and only then will we understand this reflection on the first beginning and especially on what did not occur in it.

3) The task of the Greeks: to sustain the first beginning.

We contend that it was because the Greeks sustained their task that they did not inquire into ἀλήθεια as such. Their task was the question: what are beings as such? The manner in which they asked (i.e., answered) this question must make evident why this questioning occluded for them the question of ἀλήθεια, and why this occlusion was not a restriction of their questioning but its completion, i.e., the sustaining of the first beginning.

The Greeks experienced beings as φύσις. We attempted to characterize, by way of a mere series of formulas, what resounds in this denomination of beings as such and what was conceived in a unitary way in the various directions taken by the Greek interpretation of beings as such. A really sufficient presentation would have to accomplish nothing less than an explication of the entire history of the Greek question of being, as it has been transmitted to us in the sources: beginning with the fragments of Anaximander and ending with the *Physics* and *Metaphysics* of Aristotle.

The Greeks experienced and conceived of beings as such as what is constant, in the sense of what persists in itself as well as in the sense of the enduring. Beings are for the Greeks what is present, παρεόν, over and against what is absent, ἀπεόν. They call beings the form, over and against the formless. Beings are for them the self-limiting, over and against the limitless and the dissolving. In these determinations there resides, in different ways and often hardly articulated, the basic character of standing out and standing over, emerging self-representing and standing "there," rising above, enclosing and preserving. The basic character of beings as such is this emerging, self-unfolding, and jutting-forth: the unconcealed. The fundamental character of φύσις is ἀλήθεια, and φύσις, if it is to be understood in the Greek sense and not misinterpreted by later modes of thought, must be determined on the basis of ἀλήθεια.

The Greeks inquired into beings and asked what they are as such, and they answered: unconcealedness. But this answer is a philosophical one. That means it does not finish off the questioning but, on the contrary, requires that the question be pursued and unfolded all the more: what are beings?

§33. *The beginning of thinking and the essential determination of man.*

a) The sustaining of the recognition of beings in their beingness and the essential determination of man as the perceiver of beings as such (νοῦς and λόγος).

In their great beginning, by means of which they began thinking, i.e., began the interpretation of beings as such, the Greeks would have renounced their most proper task if they had expressly questioned ἀλήθεια itself. How so? They would then not have been questioning any longer, i.e., they would not have kept themselves on the path of their questioning, one which comes to completion precisely with that answer and thereby is completely consummated. For, in order to remain within the question of being, they had to remain on the periphery of that which brings this question to its final end, namely, the answer ὄν, ἀλήθεια—since only in such a way would beings as such be unconcealed for them as constancy, presence, form, and limit. Only in such a way did the Greeks preserve for themselves the space within which the whole richness of their thinking, and consequently the determinations of beings, could unfold.

To inquire into ἀλήθεια, to question ἀλήθεια itself within the circuit and in the direction of primordial questioning, would mean to debilitate the answer as well as the questioning itself. For—as strange as it may sound—the greatest debilitation of essential questioning does not consist in being withdrawn into something more original but in being hardened in its own obviousness, petrified, and degraded into a mere formula by which it may be passed on from everyone to everyone. And in fact, the moment ἀλήθεια began to relinquish its primordial essence, i.e., unconcealedness, in favor of the correctness it itself founds, in this decisive moment, whose preparation takes place in Plato's thinking, the great philosophy of the Greeks comes to an end.

The lack of inquiry into ἀλήθεια as such is not a neglect but, quite to the contrary, the secure adherence of the Greeks to the task meted out to them. This lack of inquiry—this non-occurrence of questioning into ἀλήθεια—is the greatest. Why? Because it requires perseverance in a necessity: that is, in the task of bringing beings as such to a first recognition and thus to their most simple interpretation. It is easy to steal away quickly from something barely understood to what is new and exciting; it is seductive and effortless to evade what is simple in favor of the distractions of the multifarious and the novel. But to sustain that first recognition of beings as such in their beingness, as the Greeks did, is the most difficult and in its simplicity the most uncanny. Yet it had to occur so that in the future there might arise for the West a beginning to its thinking and man himself could know himself as a being in the midst of beings.

For what is required to recognize beings as such in their basic character of φύσις and ἀλήθεια? Nothing less than the basic attitude of the simple perception of beings in their beingness and thus in that single feature determining beings as such. Consequently, from this basic attitude of man toward beings as such, the essence of man had to be determined at the same time as that being which, in the midst of beings, lets these beings as a whole appear before itself in order to perceive and preserve them in their constancy, presence, form, and limit: in their unconcealedness. Therefore it happened that man, bound up with this beginning of thinking, was determined as that being whose distinctiveness consists in perceiving beings as such.

This perception is in Greek νοεῖν-νοῦς, and this original taking together and gathering of beings out of what they are in advance in the "one," ἕν, is in Greek λέγειν, gathering together, and λόγος. This perception is the opposite of a mere passive taking in; it is rather the constant letting emerge and letting stand forth in presence, by which beings are precisely posited back on themselves. Perception, νοεῖν, is letting φύσις hold sway or, as we may also say, the letting be of beings in what they are. Man is the perceiver of beings, the guarantor of their beingness, i.e., of their truth. Λόγος, the taking together and gathering of beings in view of the one which they are as beings, is not a subsequent piecing together of individual beings but an original anticipatory gathering, of all that can be encountered, in the *one* that beings are, whereby individual beings as such then first become visible.

b) The transformation of the primordial determination of the essence of man, as the perceiver of beings, into the determination of the essence of man as the rational animal.

Standing in the midst of beings and belonging to them, man is experienced immediately and primarily as an animal, in Greek ζῷον, in Latin *animal*. But it appears man is that animal whose distinguishing mark is to perceive beings; his basic faculty is perception and gathering, νοῦς and λόγος, or, transposed into Latin, *ratio*. *Homo est animal rationale*. We have been accustomed for a long time now to the translation, "Man is the rational animal." This is the conception of man which is still valid today; we still envision a doubling with regard to man. On the one hand, we conceive of man "biologically" as an animal, and on the other hand we appeal to his reason and rationality and make reason, "logic," the norm of his action. We consider man simply as a member of the human race, yet we require his politics to be "rational and logical." Man is the rational animal. We accept that as so obvious that it never occurs to us to think that this interpretation of man could very well have its origin in a certain particular beginning, and that means at the same time that it could have distanced itself in the meanwhile very far from that origin and could actually be something utterly questionable instead of obvious.

How far removed is this rational animal, this understanding of man's essence, from the primordial rank which thought at its beginning assigned to him? We can recapture nothing anymore of this beginning, i.e., of this necessity. For the primordial determination of man as the perceiver and preserver of beings was soon abandoned. Perception became reason, and this in turn became a faculty of a soul belonging to a body. All this itself became merely a part of beings and an occurrence within beings. In Christianity, the soul gradually became the soul of the single individual, whose otherworldly salvation dominated everything else, a salvation which becomes certain only in faith and not in *ratio*. Man and human reason are not even any longer an occurrence within beings but, together with beings themselves, are now only creatures and something created, delivered over to a fleeting and not genuine sojourn on earth. Of that perceiver and preserver of beings, nothing more remains.

And yet, in its separation from faith, reason once again makes itself autonomous through a self-interpretation, a new one, no longer in the primordial manner but in a way determined by Christianity. Reason assumes for itself the planning, constructing, and making of the world. Beings are no longer φύσις in the Greek sense but "nature," i.e., that which is captured in the planning and projects of calculation and placed in the chains of anticipatory reckonings. Reason now becomes ever more rational, and all beings turn out to be its contrivances, this word understood in an essential and not in a derogatory way. Man becomes ever more inventive and clever but at the same time more common and smaller. The occasions and the possibilities in which man brings his contrivances into play become limitless by virtue of these very contrivances. All this does not exclude, but precisely requires, that everything calculating reason posits over and against itself as limit, namely the a-rational, i.e., what can no longer be calculated by it, gains validity in reason's own way, precisely within the compass of its contrivances. The more frantic the contrivances and calculations of reason, the stronger and the more widespread is the cry for lived experience. Both are excessive and are mutually exchangeable. What is more, the contrivances, e.g., the gigantic accomplishments of technology, become themselves the greatest "lived experience," and the lived experiences seek the form of a contrivance. A boxing match is a "lived experience," but surely not for the boxers themselves; they have no lived experience, but at the limit they still box; the lived experience resides in the spectators, and what is lived is the entire display of a grand-production theater. The lived experience becomes a contrivance; let us reflect a moment on what has been put together in the term "confessional front," a term which is not merely due to the process of forming it [*denken wir einmal einen Augenblick nach, was im Wort "Bekenntnisfront" sich zusammengefunden hat, und dass es zu diesem Wort, nicht nur zum Vorgang kommt*].

The lived experience as our contrivance, and the latter itself as a lived experience—what arises in this process as a whole cannot be attributed to any one individual but is the process in which man, conscious of himself, and operating, as the "rational animal," draws the ultimate consequences of his "culture" and "civilization": the most extreme distancing from his primordially established position with regard to beings. It is one and the same process that the original essence of truth could not be retained and that historical man everywhere comes to his end along with his contrivances and lived experiences. No wonder that for us today only rarely and with difficulty does it become clear what occurred in the beginning of Western thinking *as* beginning.

§34. *The need and the necessity of our inquiry into unconcealedness itself on the basis of a more original understanding of the first beginning.*

The adherence of the Greeks to the beginning, to an inquiry into beings as such, and their adherence to the first answer, to the unfolding of what it opens up, hence their lack of inquiry into truth, are not omissions or failures but testimony to the power of the Greeks to be equal to a necessity. If *we* now ask, and perhaps must ask, what this unconcealedness itself is, then our inquiry cannot be a mere making up for an omission. Then what must it be, if it is the preparation for the occurrence of something not yet come to pass? What must our questioning be at least and at first, and indeed by necessity? It must *again* be a necessity and even again a beginning, but a different one.

Why are we asking the question of the essence of truth? Only because there is something to "criticize" in the previous conception of truth? That would be a shallow and pitiful reason. But then where is the necessity, i.e., as we put it, where is the need? The need and the necessity are peculiar and unique precisely in that they remain at first concealed to us, making it seem as if our thinking were subject to no need at all, as if we could and should continue to ramble on blissfully in the previous philosophy, i.e., misuse it recklessly and mix it all up, provided we now only apply the racial to it and give the whole a correct political face. This is not to say that these are inessential for our reflection, but what is still more essential is that we know or learn to know that great tasks require a great preparation and a still greater investment if they are to be preserved in their dignity.

We must bring ourselves explicitly into confrontation with our need, which we can do only if we face up to an essential need and its necessity and for that purpose first provide our eyes with visual power. If we cannot supply this from our own resources, then we must seek it, and will be able to find it, solely where once, and only once, a beginning had begun. We must try to understand the beginning of Western thinking in this regard in a *still* more original way.

The primordial history of the essence of truth gives rise to truth as the essence of beings themselves, as unconcealedness. This primordial positing of the essence, which is the task assigned to the beginning of the beginning, excludes an inquiry into ἀλήθεια itself. It is now clear that this lack of questioning originated out of the necessity to present, to preserve, and to unfold, once and for all, beings in their beingness. What need gave rise to this necessity? In any event, something necessary emerged for the Greeks, having nothing to do with the comportment of some individual or other, nor with the comportment of a society, but which ignited the beginning of a history, indeed of *the* history in which we are still located.

To be sure, it would be erroneous and infantile to think that the ones who had to begin this beginning were aware of it in the same retrospective way as we who have come after. For supposing this knowledge were alive then, even if only in vague surmises, the necessity of the task would have forfeited its greatness and its essentiality. For everything necessary that is supported by a known goal is thereby already tainted in its unconditionality and purity. The necessary, in its greatest form, always exists without the crutches of the why and the wherefore and without the support of the whereunto and the thereunto. In such necessity, then, a pre-eminent need must be pressing, so that what is necessary might be experienced and endured.

RECAPITULATION

1) The rigor and inner order of questioning in distinction to the systematization of a system.

In developing the question of truth it is important to stress again and again that everything depends on the *course* of our procedure. But that is not meant in the usual sense; i.e., it does not mean that the "systematic context" is to be kept in view so that all the particulars might be integrated correctly. For what is at issue is not a systematic doctrine of truth or a discussion of theses on the essence of truth which are supposed to coalesce into a doctrinal system. The epoch of philosophical "systems" is gone for ever—not because the material of knowledge has swollen so enormously that it can no longer be ordered or even surveyed, but because the very essence of knowledge has been transformed, above all in distinction and opposition to modern knowledge, which alone in itself and for itself demands "systematization." In the great beginning of Occidental thinking, there were (and this indeed by necessity) not yet systems and after the end of this first beginning there will no longer be systems. Why? Because a deeper necessity will rule thinking and questioning and because their inner order and rigor will be concealed to the seemingly unsurpassable (because it is transparent) completeness of a system. A system is the highest form of knowledge only under two conditions:

1. if and as long as all things that can be known, beings as such, are determined according to the guiding line of thinking;

2. if and as long as thinking founds itself upon ultimate principles concerning itself and determines all foundation as a deduction from these principles.

Yet even if both these conditions have already been shaken, the rigor of questioning and its course are by no means therefore submerged. It is just that the rigor and the way of procedure can now no longer be ruled by the systematization of a system.

In the unfolding of the question of truth, everything depends on the course of our procedure. The consequential fact that for centuries the conception of knowledge was determined in terms of modern science is the reason that philosophy can free itself only with great difficulty from the trammels of scientific systematization. That is to say, everything which does not appear to be a scientific treatment of an object or of a range of objects is taken to be "psychology," i.e., a description of the way philosophical thinking is "lived." There may very well be such descriptions; the philosophy of Nietzsche, to a large extent and in almost everything he himself published, can be misinterpreted along these lines.

2) Historical reflection on the necessity of the first beginning; acquisition of the norms for the necessity of our own question of truth.

If here in these lectures we say so little about the essence of truth itself and present no theory of truth but instead linger constantly over the questioning of this question of truth, then it seems we are dealing more with the "lived experience" of the question of truth than with the essence of truth. Nevertheless, this course of our procedure is neither a systematization of the problem of truth nor a psychology of its problematization. What is it then? A designation will not accomplish anything if we do not understand what is transpiring here.

The short critical discussion of the traditional concept of truth passed over into a historical reflection on the beginning of Western thought. This reflection sees itself now led to the point of thinking through the necessity of that questioning in the accomplishment of which ἀλήθεια, the unconcealedness of beings, truth, once came to knowledge, without itself becoming a question. Our historical reflection must ponder the necessity of the question of truth. This necessity is not an object of psychology; it is something else entirely. The necessity of the question of truth is rather that which decides about the "content" the essential determination of truth must have in the future. Our reflection proceeds in a completely different way than any systematization of the issues in the question of truth.

The reflection on the necessity of the question of truth decides its originality and essentiality. It decides whether, and how, that which in the beginning blazed as ἀλήθεια, to be extinguished soon thereafter, can once more become the glowing fire of the hearth of our existence [*Dasein*]. A precondition is that we be capable of thinking the essence of ἀλήθεια correctly. Our historical reflection has therefore pointed to something whose full bearing we cannot yet appreciate: namely, that truth was in the beginning the basic character of beings themselves. Which means at the same time that truth is to be known and thought in connection with the question of beings as such. But this question is the beginning of Western thought. And that implies that the necessity of the knowledge of truth goes hand in hand with the necessity of this beginning. Only in reflection on it do we acquire the sufficient norms for the necessity which must determine *our* questioning of truth, if this questioning is not to degenerate immediately into an indifferent dismembering of the concept of truth or into a mere substitution of a transformed doctrine for the traditional one, without having prepared what is most indispensable: a complete transformation of the style of thinking and questioning.

Now it has been shown finally that the question of the Greeks, the primordial question about beings as such, is of such a kind that it precludes an inquiry into ἀλήθεια as such. For unconcealedness is the determination of beings that in general and in advance constitutes the field of view within which become possible the manifestation of the characters of beings we mentioned and hence the fulfillment of the question of beings. In order to bring into view what resides in a visual field, the visual field itself must precisely light up first, so that it might illuminate what resides within it; however, it cannot and may not be seen explicitly. The field of view, ἀλήθεια, *must* in a certain sense be overlooked.

The first task was then to apprehend beings as beings, to install the pure recognition of beings as such, and nothing more. This was quite enough if we consider what was simultaneously grounded with it: the primordial determination of man as that being which, in the midst of beings as a whole, lets beings hold sway in their unconcealedness. This letting hold sway is accomplished by exhibiting beings in their forms and modes of presence and by preserving beings therein—occurrences in which poetry as well as painting and sculpture, the act that founds a state, and the worshipping of the gods first obtain their essence, bringing these essences into being historically and *as* history by their words and works, actions and raptures, assaults and downfalls.

3) The origin of the apprehension of man as the rational animal out of an inability to sustain the first beginning.

The beginning of the determination of man on the basis of his relation to beings as such was only a first inception and did not remain the beginning. What followed was incapable of adhering to this grounding of the essence of man in its primordiality, i.e., to create it ever more originally. Therefore it had to be pointed out briefly how the subsequent and now ordinary apprehension of man as rational animal originated from an inability to sustain that great beginning in which man had to bring himself before beings as such and had to be a being in the midst of beings.

We have exposed the most extreme and for us today the most visible developments of this history of the determination of the essence of man not in order to begin a sterile "critique of culture" or the like, nor even just to portray the "contemporary situation" of man. On the contrary, it is entirely and solely as connected to the question of truth and the history of its essence that we have referred to the distance between today's universally common conception of man and its beginning. For if now on the basis of a preparation which has lasted centuries, and was especially accomplished in the modern period, beings have become a contrivance of reason, of a reason which in principle nothing may resist, and if thereby this reason, as a being, appeals to lived experience, and if furthermore it should happen that the contrivance fails and "cites" destiny, then this reference to the contrivance and to the lived experience is naming only the two poles between which the ordinary conception of truth—correctness—oscillates.

The determination of truth as correctness is not the indifferent and innocuous theory of a scholastic "logic" which has been obsolete for ages. Correctness is the calculable adjustment and adaptation of all human behavior to the end of contrivances. Whatever resists these contrivances will be crushed. Yet correctness, in its effect and its success, is appropriated, preserved as a possession, and carried over into use and profit through lived experience. At the beginning of modern thought, Descartes for the first time posited the certainty of the ego, a certainty in which man is made secure of beings as the object of his representations. Now this certainty is the germ of what today, as "lived experience," constitutes the basic form of being human. It is one of the ironies of history that our age has discovered—admittedly, very late—the need to refute Descartes, and takes issue with him and his intellectualism by appealing to "lived experience," whereas lived experience is only a base descendent of the Cartesian *cogito ergo sum*.

We conclude from this allusion that the conception of man is tied to his position within truth and toward truth and that conversely the status of the question of truth, i.e., above all, the forgetting and disregarding of this question, always corresponds to a determined self-comprehension of man and of his relation to beings as such. Admittedly, this does not yet decide anything about the genuine character of the essential relation between truth and man. Above all, we may not understand the transformation of the self-understanding of man psychologically or in terms of the history of culture. These psychological, moral, and cultural transformations all move within one single constant comprehension of man—a constancy that has now been shaken and requires a first great transformation. This can only be appreciated on the basis of the relation of man to beings as such and to their truth. It follows that this transformation is rarer than we might think and that it has its most concealed but at the same time most powerful ground in the conception of beings as such and in the necessity of this conception.

Assuming that we are facing an essential transformation of the essence of truth and, in union with that, a transformation of the position of man within beings and toward beings, then this transformation can only arise from a necessity, one equal to the necessity of the beginning. Those who are preparing this transformation must be ready for such a necessity. This readiness can only be generated through a knowledge of the necessity. Such knowledge, which is not a mere handling of cognitions, has a transformative power and grows out of reflection—for us here out of reflection on the necessity of the questioning in whose circuit and as whose visual field the essence of truth first shone as ἀλήθεια, i.e., out of reflection on the character of the necessity of the beginning of Western thinking. Every necessity, however, emerges, according to its type, out of a need.

Chapter Five

The Need and the Necessity of the First Beginning and the Need and the Necessity of an Other Way to Question and to Begin

§35. *The distress of not knowing the way out or the way in, as a mode of Being. The untrodden time-space of the between.*

What sort of need held sway in the necessity to put in motion the beginning of Western thinking? And what do we understand here by "need"? "Need" is redolent of misery and complaint, it connotes deprivation and requirement, and on the whole it means lack, absence, "away," "not." Not every negation is negative in a depreciatory sense. Silence, for example, means the absence, the "away," and the "not" of noise and disturbance. But here we are just interpreting something original as negative with the aid of the negative, namely, noise and disturbance, without considering the essence of "not" and "no." Not everything negative needs to be deficient and certainly not miserable and lamentable. We have the habit of interpreting need and care only on the basis of our everyday surrounding world of what is disturbing, lamentable, and burdensome; i.e., we make our griefs and afflictions the measure of things. This habit of ours is so ineradicable that it apparently has an exclusive claim to justification, yet we must ever anew attempt to win back, or, perhaps, first develop, for our language a hidden power of naming the essential.

If we speak of need as that which makes needful the highest form of necessity, we are not referring to misery and lack. Nevertheless, we are thinking of a *not,* a negative. But we know little enough of the negative and the "no," for example in forms of refusal, deferment, and failure. Yet all that is not nothingness but is at most (if not something higher still) its opposite. It never enters the field of view of our calculating reason that a no and a not may arise out of a surplus or abundance, may be the highest gift, and as this not and no may infinitely, i.e., essentially, surpass every ordinary yes. And that is all to the good. For reason would "explain" it according to the principles of logic, whereby both affirmation and denial exist, but the yes has the priority since it posits and thus acknowledges something present at hand. What is present and at hand counts as a being. Therefore it is difficult for us, wherever we encounter something apparently "negative," not only to see in it the "positive" but also to conceive something more original, transcending that distinction. Here, where we are reflecting on the need of the necessity of the beginning, only the most profound understanding of the essence of need will suffice.

The need we have in mind arises from the distress of not knowing the way out or the way in; but that is by no means to be understood as a perplexity in some particular circumstances or other. What then is it? Not knowing the way out or the way in: that is to say, out of and into that which such knowing first opens up as an untrodden and ungrounded "space." This space (time-space)—if we may so speak of it here—is that "between" where it has not yet been determined what being is or what non-being is, though where by the same token a total confusion and undifferentiation of beings and non-beings does not sweep everything away either, letting one thing wander into another. This distress, as such a not knowing the way out of or into this self-opening "between," is a mode of "Being," in which man arrives or perhaps is thrown and for the first time experiences—but does not explicitly consider—that which we are calling the "in the midst" of beings.

This distress explodes beings, still veiled as such, in order to make the space of the "in the midst" of beings able to be occupied and founded as a possible standpoint of man. This distress—here barely intimated by speaking of it as a not knowing the way out or the way in—is the casting asunder of what will be determined forthwith as beings in their beingness over and against non-beings, assuming that the distress makes needful in man a necessity corresponding to it.

The distress we are speaking of is therefore by no means indeterminate but is very determined in its needfulness, in that it provides to thinking its essential space, and indeed does nothing else than that. For thinking means here to let beings emerge in the decisiveness of their Being and to let them stand out before oneself, to perceive them as such and thereby to name them in their beingness for the first time.

This distress—the not knowing the way out of or the way into the "in the midst," itself ungrounded, of still undifferentiated beings and non-beings—is not a lack and not a deprivation but is the surplus of a gift which, however, is more difficult to bear than any loss. This distress—we are saying—is a character of Being and not of man, as if this distress could arise "psychically" in man as a "lived experience" and have its proper place in him. On the contrary, man himself first arises out of this distress, which is more essential than he himself, for he is first determined by it.

This distress pertains to the truth of Being itself. It possesses its highest gift in being the ground of the necessity toward the highest possibilities, on the path of which man in his creations surpasses himself and returns through beings to the truth of Being.

§36. *The need of primordial thinking and how this need compels man dispositionally into the basic disposition of wonder (θαυμάζειν).*

The distress we are speaking of determines man by determining him through and through. Here, to be sure, a misunderstanding immediately insinuates itself, to the effect that the dispositions would be something man "has," dependent either on external conditions and circumstances or on inner states of the body, whereas in truth, i.e., understood on the basis of the essence of Being (as appropriating event), the dispositions have man and consequently determine him in various ways, even in his corporeality. A disposition can confine man in his corporeality as in a prison. Yet it can also carry him through corporeality as one of the paths leading out of it. In each case the world is brought to man in a different way; in each case his self is differently opened up and resolved with regard to beings.

To say it still more essentially:[1] the previous conception of man, i.e., the biological and psychological conception, would misinterpret what we have just said and would maintain that disposition is but a human capacity, though to be sure a very important one and perhaps one not yet sufficiently appreciated; a correct understanding of disposition, however, leads in fact to a surpassing of this very conception of man. We sometimes say that we have been transported *into* this or that disposition. In truth, i.e., understood on the basis of the original essence of Being, it is rather the reverse: it is the disposition that transports, transports us into this or that basic relation to beings as such. More precisely, disposition is what transports us in such a way that it co-founds the time-space of the transporting itself.

We cannot yet ask how this transporting is to be understood. But this question is an essential track within our question of openness as such (ex-istence) [(*Da-sein*)].

In view of the essence of our need, this is what we have to think in the first place: as disposing, the distress, the not knowing the way out or the way in, does not simply compel us into already determined relations to beings, ones already opened up and interpreted in their beingness; on the contrary, it compels us first of all into that "between," that "in the midst of," in whose space and time beings as a whole can be determined in their beingness. This need of primordial thinking, as we mean it here, can affectively compel us only in an essential disposition, or, as we say, in a basic one.

Finally, it might be claimed that our comments on need and disposition are merely latter-day "fantasies" and ultimately, in spite of everything, merely "psychological" opinions about the wholly unknown psychology of the early Greek thinkers. There is indeed not enough resistance to be found today against this misinterpretation, and there will not be enough even in the future, for these misinterpretations, which are always possible, will

1. On the essence of disposition see *Sein und Zeit, Gesamtausgabe, Bd.* 2, and above all the lecture course on Hölderlin: *Hölderlins Hymnen "Germanien" und "Der Rhein," Gesamtausgabe, Bd.* 39.

become impossible only on the basis of an essential transformation of thinking and questioning, and the necessary carrying out of that is now scarcely underway.

Yet our reflection on the necessity and the need of the beginning of Western thinking might prove a little less "fantastic" if we recall that the Greek thinkers themselves say that the origin of philosophy—hence the origin of what they began—is θαυμάζειν, or, as we translate, wonder. μάλα γὰρ φιλοσόφου τοῦτο τὸ πάθος, τὸ θαυμάζειν· οὐ γὰρ ἄλλη ἀρχὴ φιλοσοφίας ἢ αὕτη.[1] διὰ γὰρ τὸ θαυμάζειν οἱ ἄνθρωποι καὶ νῦν καὶ τὸ πρῶτον ἤρξαντο φιλοσοφεῖν.[2] (φιλοσοφία: ἐπιστήμη τῶν πρώτων ἀρχῶν καὶ αἰτιῶν θεωρητική).[3] Thus the origin of philosophy is a disposition? But to what extent is wonder what disposes and determines, and consequently the mode of compelling of the need we have spoken of, and therefore the way this need itself exists and incorporates man, in order to transport him, through this incorporation, into a basic disposition, into the not knowing the way out or the way in? (This not knowing became, at the end of the great Greek philosophy, in Aristotle, a component of the process of philosophizing, and today we have made of it an empty formula of pedantry.) If we wish to understand θαυμάζειν as this wonder, then we must in advance maintain strictly that the task is to clarify *the* basic disposition of the beginning of thinking. Therefore to adhere to the common representation of the meaning of θαυμάζειν cannot suffice; indeed, it will lead us into error.

It has long been known that the Greeks recognized θαυμάζειν as the "beginning" of philosophy. But it is just as certain that we have taken this θαυμάζειν to be obvious and ordinary, something that can be accomplished without difficulty and can even be clarified without further reflection. For the most part, the usual presentations of the origin of philosophy out of θαυμάζειν result in the opinion that philosophy arises from curiosity. This is a weak and pitiful determination of origin, possible only where there

1. Plato, *Theatetus. Platonis Opera*, ed. J. Burnet, vol. I, Oxford 1900. 155D 2ff. ["This is the great passion of the philosopher: wonder. There is no other beginning of philosophy than this."—Tr.]

2. Aristotle, *Metaphysica*, A 2, 982b 11ff. ["For it is precisely through wonder that people today and at the beginning began to philosophize"—Tr.]

3. Cf. ibid., A 2, 982b 8ff. ["Philosophy: theoretical knowledge of the first principles and causes"—Tr.]

has never been any reflection on what is supposed to be determined here in its origin. Indeed, we consider ourselves relieved of such reflection, precisely because we think that the derivation of philosophy out of curiosity also determines its essence. Thus we fail to realize how decisively the reference to θαυμάζειν as the origin of philosophy indicates precisely the inexplicability of philosophy, inexplicability in the sense that here in general to explain and the will to explain are mistakes.

A principal reason for the ordinary misinterpretation of θαυμάζειν is again the usual procedure of making the common understanding of the meaning of the word θαυμάζειν a norm for interpretation. For in this word is thought, as in every essential word of every language that creates history, a common as well as a pre-eminent content and meaning—in this case a disposition and an attitude. To what extent is θαυμάζειν, wonder, a basic disposition—one that transports into the beginning of genuine thinking and thoroughly determines it? In order to have a general guideline for our reflection on θαυμάζειν as a basic disposition, we will indeed begin with the ordinary concept. But our purpose is not to distinguish lexically and count up the various meanings of the word. What we want to see instead is something of the inner multiplicity of the disposition in question.

§37. *The ordinary concept of wonder as guideline for a reflection on θαυμάζειν as a basic disposition.*

a) Amazement and marvelling.

We shall not begin with wonder but with the wondrous, θαυμαστόν. The wondrous is for us in the first place something that stands out and therefore is remarkable; for the most part it also has the character of the exceptional, unexpected, surprising, and therefore exciting. A better name for this would be the curious or the marvelous, something that arouses the desire for amazement, engages it, and sustains it, specifically in such a way that it makes the search for ever new things of this kind more ardent. The marvelling and the amazement always adhere to something conspicuously unusual; this is extracted from the usual and set over against it. Thus the known, the understandable, and the explicable here form a background not further attended to, from which the marvelous emerges and is drawn away. Amazement is a certain inability to explain and ignorance of the reason. This inability to explain, however, is not by any means equivalent to a determination and a declaration that the explanation and the reason are not available. On the contrary, the not being able to explain is first and essentially a kind of being caught up in the inexplicable, being struck by it; and upon closer inspection the amazement does precisely not want to have the marvelous explained but instead wants to be teased and fascinated by the inexplicable as what is other, surprising, and uncommon in opposition to what is commonly known, boring, and empty. Nevertheless, amazement is always a determinate and singular event, a particular occurrence, a unique circumstance, and is always set off against a dominating determinate background of what is precisely familiar and ordinary.

Amazement and marveling have various degrees and levels and discover what they seek in the most diverse domains of beings. The more arbitrary, changeable, and even unessential, though indeed striking, the marvelous happens to be, the more does it satisfy amazement, which is always vigilant for opportunities and desires them so as to be stimulated in its very own passion. Being struck by what is uncommon comes to pass here in such a way that what is customary is set aside and the uncommon itself becomes something familiar that bewitches and encharms. The uncommon thus obtains its own permanent character, form, and fashion. To do so it even requires an insidious habituality. We might think in passing of all the extraordinary things the cinema must offer continually; what is new every day and never happened before becomes something habitual and always the same.

RECAPITULATION

1) The negativity of the distress as a not knowing the way out or the way in. The whence and whither as the open "between" of the undifferentiatedness of beings and non-beings.

We are reflecting on the necessity of the beginning of Occidental thinking, a beginning in which the essence of truth as the basic character of beings had to flame up, only to expire once again. This reflection is a historical one. It has value not in our applying the past to ourselves but only insofar as we enter into the history of the essence of truth, i.e., insofar as we have an ear for the demand of this hidden history, for its future, by turning the essence of truth into what is most worthy of questioning and doing so on the basis of a genuine necessity. The reflection addresses the necessity of our question of truth, out of which alone the direction and the domain of the questioning are determined, as well as what is to be founded as the essence of truth. For the character of the necessity of such questioning we require a sure eye. We will procure it only through reflection on the beginning and its necessity. This necessity springs forth out of a need. The need compels in the mode of a disposition.

Therefore it was important to say something in advance about need and disposition, in order then to characterize the basic disposition of primordial thinking as θαυμάζειν, wonder. Here we are constantly subject to the danger of making a norm out of our ordinary, habitual, and everyday experiences and interpretations of need, necessity, and disposition. We are now seeking what these same words name at the beginning of Western thought, and that is always incompatible with our everyday understanding.

Need is for us ordinarily a lack, something "negative." We immediately judge the negative, however, in a depreciatory way as the adverse pure and simple. Thus our only relation to it is defense and elimination. Now everything negative is in fact determined by a no and a not. But not every no and not, the negative, is nothingness. Need in the essential sense is indeed something negative, and yet not nothingness, which we can only be content with by eliminating or avoiding.

The need we have in mind, the ground of the necessity of primordial questioning, is a negativity in the sense of the distress of not knowing the way out or the way in. This whence and whither, as they exist in the beginning, do not constitute some definite, determinate situation, occasion, or perplexity as regards some particular comportment or relation to a determinate object and circumstance. On the contrary, the whence and whither exist no less than the open "between," in which beings and non-beings stand forth as a whole, though still in their undifferentiatedness. Since the between is the *whole* of these undifferentiated beings, there is nothing outside to which an exit would be possible. And because it is a whole that is *undifferentiated*, there is nothing to which a way might lead to a standpoint inside. What here permits neither an out nor an in oscillates back to itself in an extraordinary sense as this "between." Therefore this distress of not knowing the way out or the way in, this need, has an excess which raises it above every lack and lets something be which we have to express as the opposite of a lack, an abundance. This is the measurelessness of the undifferentiatedness between what beings as beings are as a whole and that which presses forth as inconstant, formless, and carrying away, which means here at the same time what immediately withdraws.

2) The compelling power of the need, its disposing as displacing man into the beginning of a foundation of his essence.

The need compels into the "between" of this undifferentiatedness. It first casts asunder what can be differentiated within this undifferentiatedness. Insofar as this need takes hold of man, it displaces him into this undecided "between" of the still undifferentiated beings and non-beings, as such and as a whole. By this displacement, however, man does not simply pass unchanged from a previous place to a new one, as if man were a thing that can be shifted from one place to another. Instead, this displacement places man for the first time into the decision of the most decisive relations to beings and non-beings. These relations bestow on him the foundation of a new essence. This need displaces man into the beginning of a foundation of his essence. I say advisedly *a* foundation for we can never say that it is the absolute one.

What we are now calling displacement is the essential character of what we know under the name of disposition or feeling. A deep-rooted and very old habit of experience and speech stipulates that we interpret feelings and dispositions—as well as willing and thinking—in a psychological-anthropological sense as occurrences and processes within an organism, as psychic lived experiences, ones we either have or do not have. This also means that we are "subjects," present at hand, who are displaced *into* these or those dispositions by "getting" them. In truth, however, it is the disposition that displaces us, displaces us into such and such a relation to the world, into this or that understanding or disclosure of the world, into such and such a resolve or occlusion of one's self, a self which is *essentially* a being-in-the-world.

The need compels by disposing, and this disposing is a displacing in such fashion that we find ourselves disposed (or not disposed) toward beings in a definite way.[1] If we interpret this psychologically, as lived experience, then everything is lost. That is why it is so difficult for us to gain access to the Greek world—especially its beginning—for we immediately seek "lived experiences," "personalities," and "culture"—precisely what was not there in this very great and equally short time. And that is why we are completely excluded from a real understanding of, e.g., Greek tragedy or the poetry of Pindar, for we read and hear the Greeks in psychological, even in Christian, terms. If, e.g., a Greek speaks of αἰδώς, awe, which affects ones who risk and only them, or of χάρις, the grace that donates and protects, and which in itself is severity (all these translations are miserable failures), then he is not naming lived experiences or feelings which arise in an organism and which a person might "have." The Greek indicates what he means by calling these "goddesses," or "demi-goddesses." But here again we are ready with our psychological explanations insofar as we would say that these are precisely mythical lived experiences. For myth is a particular form of lived experience, namely the irrational.

3) Θαυμάζειν as the basic disposition of the primordial thinking of the Occident.

In view of modern man's intoxication with lived experience, it is in the first place very difficult to capture a basic disposition, *the* basic disposition, which compelled the primordial thinking of the Occident into its question and let it become a necessity. Prior

1. Cf. *Being and Time* on "finding oneself disposed" [*Befindlichkeit*].

to all theories and all-encompassing systems and presentations of a futural philosophy, the task is simply to become prepared for the necessity of that question. Therefore we have to attempt to clarify the primordial basic disposition, the disposing need, even at the risk of having everything taken as a psychological explanation. For, indeed, let us not deceive ourselves: nothing is gained by making a principle out of the proposition, "The disposition has us, we do not have it." Whether or not something has been understood here will be manifest only in man's action, creation, and Being, and not in the mere pretension to be the champion of a new opinion about the essence of disposition.

The Greeks name the origin of philosophy θαυμάζειν, which we translate as "wonder." This characterization of the origin of philosophy out of marvelling—as it is also called—is often quoted and readily cited in order to account for the origin of philosophy psychologically and in that way to deprive philosophy precisely of the wondrous. All psychology intrudes in this way to disenchant and dispossess. But what is at issue here is only to raise philosophy—or any other essentially creative power—up into its inexplicability and to preserve it there, and only there, as a possible acquisition against all trivialization. To say philosophy originates in wonder means philosophy is wondrous in its essence and becomes more wondrous the more it becomes what it really is.

In order now to capture θαυμάζειν as the basic disposition of the beginning of Western philosophy, we are deliberately starting with the ordinary experiences and interpretations of what is called wonder or marvelling, so that we may expressly dispel what is ordinary from our reflection on θαυμάζειν.

The wondrous is first of all what is striking, remarkable, an exception to the habitual. We call it the curious or the amazing. To be amazed is to find oneself in face of the inexplicable, and indeed in such a way that in this disposition the inexplicability is sustained. Where amazement disposes man, he is transfixed by the curious and pursues its perpetuation, i.e., pursues its continued change, alternation, and exaggeration. For that is what distinguishes something curious: as a determinate, individual "this," it falls outside of every determinate, individual sphere of the familiar and known. By the same token, the amazing is something determinate, individual, and unusual, set off against what is determinate and usual. To be amazed is to be carried away by something particular and unusual and hence is an abandonment of what in its own sphere is particular and usual.

b) Admiration.

Admiration is different from amazement and marvelling. The admired is indeed also something unusual, and again is something individual set off against the usual. Yet it is no longer merely that which captures curiosity and surprise, or which enthralls and amazes. The unusual that provokes admiration, the admired, becomes objective explicitly *as* the unusual. The production of what is admired, the achievement by which it comes to be in the way it comes to be, is explicitly acknowledged and appreciated.

No matter how wholly and genuinely admiration may be carried away by what fulfills it, yet it always involves a certain freedom over and against what is admired. This occurs to such a degree that all admiration, despite its retreating in face of the admired, its self-deprecating recognition of the admired, also embodies a kind of self-affirmation. Admiration claims the right and the capacity to perform the evaluation which resides in the admiration and to bestow it on the admired person. The admirer knows himself—perhaps not in the ability to accomplish things, though indeed in the power to judge them—equal to the one admired, if not even superior. Therefore, conversely, everyone who allows himself to be admired, and precisely if the admiration is justified, is of a lower rank. For he subordinates himself to the viewpoint and to the norms of his admirer. To the truly noble person, on the contrary, every admiration is an offense. This is not meant to discredit admiration itself. Within its proper limits, it is necessary. Without admiration, what would become of a ski jumper or a race driver, a boxer or an actor?

What is admired is—just like the curious—in each case something unusual juxtaposed to the usual, i.e., near it and over it, such that there can be exchange, to and fro, from one to the other, because, in this juxtaposition, each needs the other.

c) Astonishment and awe.

Admiration must be distinguished from astonishment and awe. Indeed, we find here, as in the case of admiration, a characteristic retreating in face of the awesome, up to what is called dumfoundedness. But in astonishment this retreating in face of the extraordinary no longer postures as that fundamentally arrogant and self-referential evaluation and patronization found well- or ill-concealed in all admiration. In admiration there always resides an attitude that knows itself as applying to oneself as much as to the admired. Astonishment includes a decisive suspension of position-taking. The unusual is now no longer merely what is other, the exciting opposite of the usual, and it is also not merely what is acknowledged as extraordinary and made equal in rank to the admirer. Astonishment rather allows the unusual to grow, precisely as what is extraordinary, into what overgrows all usual powers and bears in itself a claim to a rank all its own. Astonishment is imbued with the awareness of being excluded from what exists in the awesome. Yet even here the astonishment is still in every case an encounter with and a being struck by a determinate individual object of awe. Hence even astonishment does not fulfill what we intend with the word wonder and what we are trying to understand as the basic disposition, the one that transports us into the beginning of genuine thinking.

§38. *The essence of wonder as the basic disposition compelling us into the necessity of primordial thinking.*

What we call, in an emphatic sense, wonder, and claim to be the essence of ϑαυμάζειν, is different, essentially different, from all types and levels of amazement, admiration, and astonishment. We will attempt to clarify in thirteen points the essence of wonder, i.e., *the* basic disposition compelling us into the necessity of primordial questioning. All the previously mentioned modes of marvelling—if we may collect them under this title—have one thing in common throughout all their differentiations, namely that in them a determinate individual object stands out as being unusual and distinguishes itself with regard to an equally determinate sphere of what is experienced precisely as usual. The unusual, as other, is in each case opposed to the usual, and all amazement, admiration, and awe are a turning away from the usual, thereby leaving it alone and bypassing it in its usualness. Now what about wonder?

a) In wonder what is most usual itself becomes the most unusual.

The usual and the most usual—precisely the most usual whose usualness goes so far that it is not even known or noticed in its usualness—this most usual itself becomes in wonder what is most unusual.

b) In wonder what is most usual of all and in all, in whatever manner this might be, becomes the most unusual.

The most usual, which arises in wonder as the unusual, is not this or that, something particular that has shown itself as objective and determinate in some specific activity or individual consideration. In wonder, what is most usual of all and in all, i.e., *everything*, becomes the most unusual. Everything has in everything at first the most usual to which attention is not paid and which, if it is glimpsed, is not explicitly heeded. Everything bears in everything the most usual, for this exists everywhere, altogether, and in every way. Everything in what is most usual (beings) becomes in wonder the most unusual in this one respect: that it is what it is. This implies:

c) The most extreme wonder knows no way out of the unusualness of what is most usual.

For the most extreme wonder, anything whatsoever as such and everything as everything become the most unusual. Thus this wonder no longer adheres to this or that, from which it could still explain the unusualness of the usual and thereby could dispel its unusualness and turn it into something ordinary. But by extending into the most extreme unusualness, wonder no longer encounters anything that could offer it an escape. It no longer knows the way out but knows itself solely as being relegated to the most unusual of the usual in everything and anything: beings as beings.

d) Wonder knows no way into the unusualness of what is most usual.

While wonder must venture out into the most extreme unusualness of everything, it is at the same time cast back wholly on itself, knowing that it is incapable of penetrating the unusualness by way of explanation, since that would precisely be to destroy it. Wonder knows no way into the unusualness of what is most usual of all, as little as it knows a way out—it is simply placed before the unusualness of the usual, in the midst of the usual in everything.

e) Wonder as between the usual and the unusual.

Not knowing the way out or the way in, wonder dwells in a between, between the most usual, beings, and their unusualness, their "is." It is wonder that first liberates this between as the between and separates it out. Wonder—understood transitively—brings forth the showing of what is most usual in its unusualness. Not knowing the way out or the way in, between the usual and the unusual, is not helplessness, for wonder as such does not desire help but instead precisely opens up this between, which is impervious to any entrance or escape, and must constantly occupy it. Wonder does not divert itself from the usual but on the contrary adverts to it, precisely as what is the most unusual of everything and in everything. Insofar as this disposition turns to the whole and stands in the whole, it is called a basic disposition.

f) The eruption of the usualness of the most usual in the transition of the most usual into the most unusual. What alone is wondrous: beings *as* beings.

We said that in wonder what is most usual of everything and of anything, thus everything itself, becomes the most unusual. This makes it seem as if the most usual were already somehow experienced in advance and known in its usualness. But that is precisely not the case, for then what is most usual would indeed no longer be the most usual. The usualness of the most usual first erupts the moment the most usual becomes the most unusual. In this transition the most usual first steps forth separately in its usualness *and* in its unusualness, such that these then appear precisely as such. In this way, wonder now opens up what alone is wondrous in it: namely, the whole as the whole, the whole as beings, beings as a whole, that they are and what they are, beings *as* beings, *ens qua ens*, τὸ ὄν ᾗ ὄν, What is meant here by the "as," the *qua*, the ᾗ, is the "between" that wonder separates out, the open of a free space hardly surmised and heeded, in which beings come into play as such, namely as the beings they are, in the play of their Being.

g) Wonder displaces man into the perception of beings as beings, into the sustaining of unconcealedness.

Wonder is the casting asunder of this free space, such that at the same time it displaces the wonderer into the midst of what was cast apart. Wondering man is the one *moved* by wonder, i.e., displaced by this basic disposition into an essence determined by it. Wonder displaces man out of the confusing irresolvability of the usual and the unusual into the first resolution of his essence. As disposed in wonder, he can perceive nothing else than beings as beings. That is to say, as moved by wonder, man must gain a foothold in the acknowledgment of what has erupted, and he must see it in a productive seeing of its inscrutable disclosure, and must experience and sustain ἀλήθεια, unconcealedness, as the primordial essence of beings. For what we must above all come to know is that ἀλήθεια, unconcealedness, is for primordial Greek thinking the essence of Being itself. Unconcealedness means an emergent coming forth, a coming to presence in the open. Ἀλήθεια, unconcealedness (we say much too emptily "truth"), does not first come to beings insofar as we acknowledge them. On the contrary, in unconcealedness beings *as* beings, i.e., as open presences, approach man and displace him into the open of unconcealedness and thus place him into the essence of one who[1] perceives and gathers in the open and thereby first experiences the hidden and closed as such.

h) Wonder as a basic disposition belongs to the most unusual.

Wonder displaces man into and before beings as such. Such displacing is the proper disposing of the basic disposition. We call it the *basic* disposition because in disposing man it displaces him into that on which and in which word, work, and deed, as historical, can be *based* and history can begin. The basic disposition, however, can neither be simply brought about by man's will nor is it the effect of a cause issuing from beings and operating on man. This displacement is beyond explanation, for all explanation here necessarily falls short and comes too late, since it could only move within, and would have to appeal to, something that was first encountered as unconcealed in the displacement that casts asunder. All explanation is directed to some being, already unconcealed, from which alone an explanatory cause can be drawn. The basic disposition of wonder displaces man into the realm where the most usual, yet still as such unthought (beings), are established in their most proper unusualness, namely the one of their Being, and where beings as such then become the most worthy of questioning. The basic disposition itself belongs to what is most unusual and most rare. Insofar as man can at all by himself bring about a relation to it, he can make himself *ready* for the unconditional necessity that holds sway in this disposition and admits of no escape. Wonder is the basic disposition that primordially disposes man into the beginning of thinking, because, before all else, it displaces man into that essence whereby he then finds himself in the midst of beings as such and as a whole and finds himself caught up in them.

i) Analysis of wonder as a retrospective sketch of the displacement of man into beings as such.

This analysis of wonder, as a basic disposition compelling us into the first beginning, should not be misunderstood to the effect that the disposition would be, in its primordiality, a conscious

1. [Reading *der* for *das*, following the second edition.—Tr.]

one. On the contrary, the uniqueness of the unconditioned domination of this disposition and of its compelling character involves, as is the case with every basic disposition, the highest simplicity of complete incomprehensibility and its unconditioned expansion. Our analysis—should we want to name it such—is not a dissection in the sense of an explanatory dissolution into a manifold of components. It is simply an attempt at a retrospective sketch of the simplicity and incomprehensibility of that displacement of man, into beings as such, which comes to pass as wonder. And the latter remains exactly as ungraspable as the beginning itself, toward which it compels.

The misinterpretation of this retrospective sketch as a dissection is, to be sure, all the more tempting the longer we have been habituated, even here, precisely in this pre-eminent realm, to take everything "psychologically," as occurrences of lived experiences "in" the human soul. Whereas, on the contrary, man himself is first disposed toward the beginning through the occurrence of this displacement and is thereby determined as a primordial perceiver of beings as such.

j) The sustaining of the displacement prevailing in the basic disposition of wonder in the carrying out of the necessity of the question of beings as such.

All this contains a clue indicating where we might find the necessity of the attitude of primordial thinking. The basic disposition of θαυμάζειν compels us to a pure acknowledgment of the unusualness of the usual. The purest acknowledgment of what is most unusual is fulfilled, however, in the questioning that asks what the most usual itself might be, such that it can reveal itself as what is most unusual.

But is this questioning not precisely intrusiveness and curiosity, hence that which most eludes all pure acknowledgment? To be sure it is, but only if we understand this questioning as a part of our everyday comportment and dealings and as a part of the rage to make explanation the measuring rod for the determination of the essence of thoughtful questioning. But thoughtful questioning is not the intrusive and rash curiosity of the search for explanations; it is the tolerating and sustaining of the unexplainable as such, despite being overwhelmed by the pressure of what reveals itself. The sustaining of the unexplainable seeks to perceive only that which the unconcealed reveals in its unconcealedness: namely, presence, constancy, self-installation in a form, self-limitation in a look. The sustaining of the basic disposition is not a melting into or a vague and empty wallowing in "feelings"; on the contrary, it is the carrying out of the necessity of the question of beings as such in their region.

RECAPITULATION

1) The basic disposition of wonder versus related kinds of marvelling.

We are reflecting on the essence of *the* basic disposition, the one that was compelling at the beginning of Western thinking. It let the question of beings as such become a necessity, though in such a way that it precluded a direct inquiry into ἀλήθεια. This basic disposition is wonder. We have been trying to clarify its essence, its type of disposing. The disposing of a basic disposition is the transformative displacing of man into beings and before them. In order to draw out with sufficient clarity the manner of this disposing in wonder, we attempted to distinguish this basic disposition from related, though essentially different, kinds of marvelling. We mentioned and clarified some aspects of amazement, admiration, and awe. In each case the result was a different position of man: he may be captured by the amazing and get lost in it, he may posit himself as free in relation to the admired, in a certain sense equal to it if not even superior, or he may submit to the awesome by holding himself back. What is common to all these modes of marvelling is that in each case, even if in different ways, a determinate individual object as something unusual is set off against a determinate sphere of the usual and the latter is put aside and for the time being abandoned. How does wonder stand versus all these?

It is precisely with regard to this relation toward the usual and the unusual that the basic disposition of wonder—as something entirely different—is easiest to clarify.

2) Sequence of steps in the characterization of wonder as a way toward the necessity of the primordial question.

We are attempting to characterize wonder in thirteen points. Reflection will show that it is not a matter of listing arbitrarily selected properties of wonder, but rather that it is a deliberate arrangement leading to the goal of our meditation: the necessity of primordial questioning, a necessity that precluded an inquiry into ἀλήθεια. This implies that only a corresponding necessity and need can be compelling toward the question of truth and hence can predetermine the essential foundation of the more original essence of truth. We have gone through the first ten points of the characterization of wonder. In wonder, something unusual is not set off against the usual, but instead wonder sets *us* before the usual itself precisely as what is the most unusual. By the same token, the usual is not this or that or some particular domain, but because wonder places us before what is most usual and the latter is constantly manifest in everything and anything in such a way that it is precisely overlooked, so everything in everything becomes the most unusual. Thus there is no way out for the wonder to escape in order from there to explain the most unusual and thereby make it again the usual. But just as little does wonder have available a way in; it cannot penetrate into and dissolve the unusual, for that would simply destroy the unusualness. Wonder does not permit a way out or a way in; instead, it displaces us before and into the unusualness of everything in its usualness. The most usual as such first steps forth in its unusualness when the latter shines in wonder. Wonder displaces us before everything in everything—that it is and is what it is—in other words, before beings as beings. While man is displaced into it, he himself is transformed into one who, not knowing the way out or the way in, has to hold fast to beings as beings in pure acknowledgment. This is the most simple and is the greatest; it is the all-decisive beginning, toward which the basic disposition compels. The acknowledgment of beings as beings, however, is only sustained in questioning what beings as such are. This question is not a desire for explanation or for the elimination of the most unusual, that beings are what they are. On the contrary, this question is an ever purer adherence to beings in their unusualness, i.e., in primordial terms, in their pure emergence, in their unconcealedness (ἀλήθεια), and in what belongs immediately to this and unfolds out of it. To sustain the basic disposition means to *carry out* the necessity of such questioning, toward which the not knowing the way out or the way in compels us. But what is meant by this carrying out as a sustaining of the basic disposition?

k) The carrying out of the necessity: a suffering in the sense of the creative tolerance for the unconditioned.

We might first interpret the carrying out of the necessity as the simple implementation of something required. We thereby understand "carrying out" as our accomplishment and the product of our contrivances. Carrying out would thus be an activity of our own action. But the carrying out of *the* necessity into which the need of the basic disposition compels, the thoughtful questioning of beings as such, is essentially suffering [*Leiden*]. Now the mere mention of this word will immediately place us once again within the sphere of a common misinterpretation. We will think in a Christian-moralistic-psychological way of a submissive acceptance, a mere bearing patiently, a renunciation of all pride. Or else we will identify this suffering with inactivity and oppose it to action. The latter immediately refers to the field of the imperial, especially if action is set against mere thought. But even if we bring reflective thinking into this distorted opposition to action, for us thinking always remains a performance and by no means something suffered. So suffering has to mean here something other than mere submission to woes. To be sure, suffering here refers to the acceptance of what overgrows man and in that way transforms him and makes him ever more tolerant for what he is supposed to grasp when he has to grasp beings as such and as a whole. The carrying out of the necessity is here a suffering in the sense of this kind of creative tolerance for the unconditioned. This suffering is beyond activity and passivity as commonly understood.

Perhaps we may interpret a fragment of the hymns of Hölderlin's later poetry in terms of this essential suffering; "perhaps"—for indeed this fragment means something still more profound, to which we are not yet equal.[1] Von Hellingrath assigns this fragment to that larger fragment which he has entitled "Out of the range of motives of the Titans."[2] It certainly belongs there, though not by reason of some special relation, but because the fragment we will cite names something that constitutes a—if not *the*—essential determination of the entire domain of the later hymns.

The verse runs as follows:

> For tremendous powers wander over the earth,
> And their destiny touches the one
> Who suffers it and looks upon it,
> And it also touches the hearts of the peoples.
>
> For a demigod must grasp everything,
> Or a man, in suffering,
> Insofar as he hears, alone, or is himself
> Transformed, surmising from afar the steed of the lord,

Renouncing a full interpretation, we will only provide a directive to the context. Hölderlin says either a demigod or a man—in suffering—must grasp everything. And the suffering is twofold: hearing, looking, perception, and letting oneself be transformed, whereby the distant surmising of the steed of the lord, the coming of the god, is opened up. Suffering: a perception or a transformation; the essential is the advertence in hearing and, together with that, a readiness for the transition into another Being.[3] In hearing, we project and extend ourselves over and into broad expanses, though in such a way that, complying with what is heard, we bring ourselves back into the gathering of our essence. Perception is something suffered in the sense of the most expansive, and at the same time the most intimate, passion. All grasping is measured according to the standard of the power for such suffering.

The grasping occurs only in suffering. Here resides for Höl-

1. Hölderlin, *Bruchstücke und Entwürfe*, No. 14. In: *Sämtliche Werke*. Ed. N. v. Hellingrath. *Bd.* IV, 2 ed. Berlin 1923. Pp. 247f., verses 18–27.

2. Ibid., pp. 215–218.

3. On "suffering" and the "suffering of the god," see the conclusion of "*Wie wenn am Feiertage*," *ibid.*, pp. 151ff.

derlin above all the freedom from everything coerced, from all coercion and calculation, from all mistaking of time, of the moment whose time has come. For how else than in the sense of this essential suffering could someone from afar surmise the god, where it is said of god:

The reflective god hates all untimely growth.[1]

After what we briefly said earlier about Hölderlin in connection with the task of reflecting on the beginning, it is certainly not an accident that we are referring to the poet in order to elucidate what we mean by "suffering" as the essential form of the carrying out of the necessity.

ι) Τέχνη as the basic attitude toward φύσις, where the preservation of the wondrous (the beingness of beings) unfolds and is established. Τέχνη maintains the holding sway of φύσις in unconcealedness.

The sustaining of the compelling basic disposition, as the carrying out of the necessity, is a suffering in the sense indicated, and that is the essence of thoughtful questioning. In such suffering there occurs a correspondence to what has to be grasped, while the one who grasps is transformed according to it. "According to it": that means that what is to be grasped (here, beings as such in their beingness) constrains the one who is grasping, constrains him to a basic position, in virtue of which the pure acknowledgment of the unconcealedness of beings can unfurl. The one who is grasping and perceiving must accord with what is to be grasped so that the latter, beings themselves, are indeed grasped, though in such a way that thereby they are precisely released to their own essence, in order to hold sway in themselves and thus to pervade man as well. Beings, which the Greeks call φύσις, must stand in ἀλήθεια. Here we again touch what is most concealed: that the grasping is a suffering.

How else could we understand the extent to which the two greatest and most renowned thinkers of the early Greek period,

1. *Ibid.*, p. 218.

Heraclitus and Parmenides, agree in their basic positions? Heraclitus claims that beings are one in λόγος—in the anticipatory gathering—and Parmenides teaches that beings are what is perceived in νοεῖν—in perception—and this *perceptual* anticipatory gathering indicates that the grasping is a suffering as a transformation of man.

Accord with what is original is therefore precisely not an assimilation in the sense that man would simply *be* φύσις. On the contrary, he is to be distinguished from it, but in a way that accords with it, i.e., in a way that adheres to its measure (adheres to φύσις), comports itself accordingly, and orders this comportment. Even if man himself is precisely not beings as a whole, nevertheless he is the one who is displaced into the midst of beings as the preserver of their unconcealedness. So this perceiving and preserving cannot be determined as φύσις but must be other: in accord with φύσις, releasing it, and yet grasping it.

What then is it? What is the basic attitude in which the preservation of the wondrous, the beingness of beings, unfolds and, at the same time, defines itself? We have to seek it in what the Greeks call τέχνη. Yet we must divorce this Greek word from our familiar term derived from it, "technology," and from all nexuses of meaning that are thought in the name of technology. To be sure, that modern and contemporary technology could emerge, and had to emerge, has its ground in the beginning and has its foundation in an unavoidable incapacity to hold fast to the beginning. That means that contemporary technology—as a form of "total mobilization" (Ernst Jünger)—can only be understood on the basis of the beginning of the basic Western position toward beings as such and as a whole, assuming that we are striving for a "metaphysical" understanding and are not satisfied with integrating technology into the goals of politics.

Τέχνη does not mean "technology" in the sense of the mechanical ordering of beings, nor does it mean art in the sense of mere skill and proficiency in procedures and operations. Τέχνη means knowledge: know-how in processes against beings (and in the encounter with beings), i.e., against φύσις. To be sure, here it is neither possible nor necessary to enter into the variations of the meaning of the word τέχνη, which are not accidental. We only have to be mindful that this word still, precisely with Plato, at times assumes the role of denoting knowledge pure and simple, and that means the perceptual relation to beings as such. Now it is clear that this perceiving of beings in their unconcealedness is not a mere gaping, that wonder is carried out rather in a procedure against beings, but in such a way that these themselves precisely show themselves. For that is what τέχνη means: to grasp beings as emerging out of themselves in the way they show themselves, in their outward look, εἶδος, ἰδέα, and, in accord with this, to care for beings themselves and to let them grow, i.e., to order oneself within beings as a whole through productions and institutions. Τέχνη is a mode of proceeding *against* φύσις, though not yet in order to overpower it or exploit it, and above all not in order to turn use and calculation into principles, but, on the contrary, to retain the holding sway of φύσις in unconcealedness. Therefore, because the pure acknowledgment of beings as such, the perception of φύσις in its ἀλήθεια, is the disposing need in the basic disposition of wonder, τέχνη and its carrying out become necessary as what is wholly other than φύσις—wholly other yet belonging to φύσις in the most essential way.

m) The danger of disturbing the basic disposition of wonder in carrying it out. Τέχνη as the ground for the transformation of ἀλήθεια into ὁμοίωσις. The loss of the basic disposition and the absence of the original need and necessity.

This basic attitude toward φύσις, τέχνη, as the carrying out of the necessity and need of wonder, is at the same time, however, the ground upon which arises ὁμοίωσις, the transformation of ἀλήθεια as unconcealedness into correctness. In other words, in carrying out the basic disposition itself there resides the danger of its disturbance and destruction. For in the essence of τέχνη, as required by φύσις itself, as the occurrence and establishment of the unconcealedness of beings, there lies the possibility of *arbitrariness*, of an unbridled positing of goals and thereby the possibility of escape out of the necessity of the primordial need.

If this happens, then in place of the basic disposition of wonder, the avidity for learning and calculation enters in. Philosophy itself then becomes one institution among others, it becomes subjected to a goal which is all the more insidious the higher it is—e.g., Plato's παιδεία, a word we badly translate as "education." Even the fact that in the *Republic* philosophers are destined to be βασιλεῖς, the highest rulers, is already an essential demotion of philosophy. While the grasping of beings, the acknowledgment of them in their unconcealedness, unfolds into τέχνη, inevitably and increasingly the aspects of beings, the "ideas," which are brought into view in such grasping, become the only standard. The grasping becomes a sort of know-how with regard to the ideas, and that requires a constant assimilation to them. At bottom, however, it is a more profound and more hidden process. It is the loss of the basic disposition, the absence of the original need and necessity, a process linked to the loss of the original essence of ἀλήθεια.

In this way, the beginning contains in itself the unavoidable necessity that, in unfolding, it must surrender its originality. This does not speak against the greatness of the beginning but in favor of it. For, would what is great ever be great if it did not have to face up to the danger of collapse and did not have to succumb in its historical consequences to this danger, only to remain all the more illuminating in its initial singularity? In the beginning, the question of beings stays within the clarity of ἀλήθεια as the basic character of beings. Ἀλήθεια itself, however, remains by necessity unquestioned. But the sustaining of the beginning position in the sense of τέχνη leads to a falling away from the beginning. Beings become, to exaggerate somewhat, objects of representations conforming to them. Now ἀλήθεια itself is also interrogated, but henceforth from the point of view of τέχνη, and ἀλήθεια becomes the correctness of representations and procedures.

§39. *The need arising from the lack of need. Truth as correctness and philosophy (the question of truth) as without need and necessity.*

Ever since truth became correctness and this essential determination of truth, in all its manifold variations, became known as the only standard one, philosophy has lacked the most original need and necessity of the beginning. After having been for a time the handmaiden of theology, philosophy was emancipated into that free domain of the development of the self-positing human capacities whose carrying out creates, cultivates, and settles what has been called "culture" ever since. Philosophy is a free unfolding of *a* human capacity, that of thinking, and hence is but one cultural asset among others. Gradually the modern period included philosophy under the concept of a "factor" of culture, a notion in which anyone who has ears to hear must hear calculations and contrivances determining in advance the Being of man in the midst of beings. And, finally, to the extent that the nineteenth century had to make culture the object of a cultural politics, philosophy became a curiosity, or what comes down to the same thing: the essence of truth became the most unquestioned and hence a matter of the highest indifference. The fact that in all so-called cultured countries of the West and of the East professors teach philosophy in colleges and universities does not contradict this state of philosophy and of the question of truth, because it does not in the least touch it.

Now there are today everywhere daydreamers and sentimental people enough, who lament this situation of philosophy and thereby posture as defenders of the endangered spirit. But what they would like is simply that philosophy become again a more appreciated cultural asset. This concern over philosophy is a mere desire to return to the tranquility of a previous age, and it is on the whole and essentially more pernicious than the complete disdain and disavowal of philosophy. For this backward-looking concern leads into error, into misconstruing the moment of Western history.

What is the significance of the fact that philosophy became a curiosity and that the essence of truth is unquestioned and an inquiry into it without necessity? And what does it mean that philosophy stands at the end of its first beginning, in a state that corresponds to the beginning—if only as a final state? Once philosophy was the most strange, the most rare, and the most unique; now it is the same, but only in the form of curiosity. Once, in the beginning of Occidental thinking, truth was unquestioned, beyond questioning, but was so in virtue of the highest need and necessity of questioning beings. Now the essence of truth is also unquestioned, the most unquestioned, but only as what is of the highest indifference within the age of the complete questionlessness of the essential. The question of truth is without necessity. This is an essential cognition which emerges only in genuine reflection. This knowledge, the taking seriously of the situation of philosophy, is alone decisive. The concern over philosophy as a cultural asset can be left to itself.

The question of truth is without necessity. In view of the reflection we have carried out on the beginning, that means that the question of truth is without need; the basic disposition, which would primordially displace man again into beings as a whole, is absent and is denied us.

Is the need absent, or is contemporary man already so enchanted by his contrivances, and so carried away by his lived experiences, that he is no longer equal to the need, assuming the essential need is not something miserable, to which we could only be ill-disposed, but is precisely the greatest?

What if the fact that we feel no need, this lack of need, would precisely express our need, one still denied us? What if our need arises out of this lack of need?

But these questions, which are not supposed to say anything and are thought rather to keep silent about everything, lead us into the place of our greatest danger: that we today bring up this need in idle talk, scarcely having mentioned it, and even convince ourselves that it is a "lived experience," without ever having been compelled by it, let alone having carried out its necessity. To encounter this danger here, we would have to reflect on the necessity of the beginning of Western thought, at whose end we are now standing.

§40. *The abandonment of beings by Being as the concealed ground of the still hidden basic disposition. The compelling of this basic disposition into another necessity of another questioning and beginning.*

From this reflection we now know that the essential need, which, as a basic disposition, compelled the primordial questioning, sprang forth from beings themselves as a whole, insofar as beings had to be acknowledged in their beingness and had to be preserved in their truth. If for us nothing less is at stake than the preparation for a transition from the end of the first beginning into another beginning, then the need which compels us to this necessity must again and *only* come out of beings as a whole, insofar as they become a question with regard to their Being.

But this already says that on the basis of the transformation of the essence of truth into correctness, *our* basic position toward beings is not any more and never again will be that of the first beginning, although it remains determined by it as a counter-thrust. Therefore the basic disposition can no longer be the one of wonder, in which beings as such with regard to their Being once emerged as the most unusual. How far we are removed from the possibility of being again displaced toward beings by this basic disposition of the beginning can easily be measured by the fact that for centuries the Being of beings, which was for the Greeks the most wondrous, has passed as the most obvious of everything obvious and is for us the most common: what everybody always knows. For who is supposed not to know what he means when he says the stone *is*, the sky *is* overcast?

Yet this may express something whose content and bearing we do not at all yet surmise, namely that we are dealing with beings as the object of contrivances and of lived experiences and thereby are not paying attention to the Being of these beings. On account of its obviousness, Being is something forgotten. The forgottenness of Being holds us in its grip, or, what comes down to the same thing, philosophy as the question of beings as such is now by necessity a mere curiosity. The forgottenness of Being dominates, i.e., it determines our relation to beings, so that even beings, that they are and what they are, remain a matter of indifference. It is almost as if beings have been abandoned by Being, and we are heedless of it, and are more heedless the greater becomes the insidious outcry over metaphysics and ontology. For that merely expresses a desire to return to the familiar past instead of working for the future even without being able to see it.

Beings *are*, but the Being of beings and the truth of Being and consequently the Being of truth are denied to beings. Beings *are*, yet they remain abandoned by Being and left to themselves, so as to be mere objects of our contrivance. All goals beyond men and peoples are gone, and, above all, what is lacking is the creative power to create something beyond oneself. The epoch of the highest abandonment of beings by Being is the age of the total questionlessness of Being.

But what if this abandonment of beings by Being were an *event* which proceeds from beings as a whole, indeed in such a way that precisely this event is the least visible and experienceable, because it is the best concealed? For precisely the progress of all contrivance and the self-certainty of all lived experience know themselves to be in such proximity to reality and life that a greater proximity can hardly be represented. What if the abandonment of beings by Being were the most hidden and most proper ground, and the essence, of what Nietzsche first recognized as "nihilism" and interpreted in terms of "morality" and the "ideal," in the fashion of the philosophy of Plato and Schopenhauer, but did not yet understand *metaphysically*? ("Metaphysically" means: in the perspective of the basic occurrence of the primordial question, the guiding question of Western philosophy, and consequently not yet in the perspective of what originally points to the domain of the genuine, renewed surpassing of nihilism.) What if the abandonment of beings by Being, that beings still "are" and yet Being and its truth remain denied to beings and consequently to man (the denial itself understood as the essence of Being), what if this event which proceeds out of beings as a whole were the concealed ground of the still veiled basic disposition which compels us into another necessity of another original questioning and beginning? What if the abandonment of beings by Being were linked to the need arising from the fact that for us the essence of truth and the question of truth are *not* yet necessary? What if the need arising from the lack of need and, on account of its hidden domination, the age of complete questionlessness, had its ground in the abandonment of beings by Being?

We must pass through this reflection in order to allow the meditation on the first beginning to become what it is: the thrust into the transition. But perhaps this reflection precisely shows us, assuming we have carried it out long enough and, above all, with sufficient preparation and insight, how little we are equal to, or can even expect, being struck by the basic disposition, which belongs to the need arising from the lack of need, to the abandonment of beings by Being. We will not be equal to it as long as we do not prepare ourselves for it and instead take refuge in the opinion that metaphysical-historical reflection paralyzes and endangers action, whereas it is precisely the genuine beginning of the future. For great surmises enter into reflection and remain there. To be sure, through such reflection we arrive at the entire ambiguity proper to a historical transition: that we have been thrust into a future but we have not been empowered to seize the thrust in a creative way and to transfer it into the form of the future, i.e., to prepare that by which alone a beginning begins, the leap into another knowledge.

§41. *The necessity held out for us: to bring upon its ground openness as the clearing of the self-concealing—the question of the essence of man as the custodian of the truth of Being.*

As regards the question of truth, this means that our discussion is without result. Since we steadfastly take into account the point of view of today and of the past, we are always waiting to be told what the essence of truth is. We await it all the more, since our discussion began with a critical reference to the openness lying at the ground of correctness and we called this openness the most worthy of questioning.

Our discussion is admittedly without result as long as we ignore everything else that was said and only look for a "new" declaration of the essence of truth and thereby determine that we have profited nothing.

But what has happened? The discussion was entitled, "Foundational issues in the *question of truth*"—a reflection on the questioning of this question. Soon we were moving more and more, and then exclusively, in a historical reflection on the beginning of Western thinking, on how there for the first time the essence of truth shone as the basic character of beings as such, on which need and basic disposition compelled into which necessity of questioning. Finally the reflection leaped over to *our* need. Did the reflection only leap to this at the end, or did it not constantly concern us and *only* us ourselves?

The "result" of our discussions—if we would speak of it at all—consists, insofar as it consists in anything, precisely in our relinquishing the search for a new doctrine and first and foremost getting to know and learning to question which historical dimensions and inner presuppositions are contained in the question of truth. Since the question of truth is the preamble for future thinking, it itself first determines the domain, the type, and the disposition of future knowledge. Therefore the first thing we have to do is to put ourselves in a position that will never again permit us to insert our discussion of the question of truth into the habitual realms of previous doctrines, theories, and systems.

The result of these "basic" discussions consists—if it must consist in something—in a *transformation* of perspectives, norms, and claims, a transformation which at the same time is nothing other than a *leap* into a more original and more simple course of essential occurrences in the history of Western thinking, a history we ourselves *are*. Only after our thinking has undergone this transformation of attitude by means of historical reflection, will we surmise, in an auspicious moment, that already in our discussions another essence of truth, and perhaps indeed only that, was at issue. For if we had not already penetrated to this point, how else could we know something of the first beginning, which in the most extreme case reveals itself only to a knowledge of what is least like it, i.e., the wholly other.

To be sure, we only hinted that the determination of the essence of truth as the correctness of an assertion, which has been valid for ages, contains something ungrounded at its foundation: the openness of beings. Certainly it was only a hint to ἀλήθεια, the unconcealedness of beings, which, as was shown, expresses less the essence of truth than it does the essence of beings. But why should ἀλήθεια not pre-announce that openness without, however, being identical with it? For the openness we have in mind can no longer be experienced as a character of the beings standing before us and around us, not to speak of the fact that to us the unique experience of the Greeks and the possible ground of our future history remain denied, precisely through the history which lies between us and the Greeks.

But perhaps something else is held out to us as a necessity: to bring the openness itself, what comes to presence in it and how that comes to presence, upon its ground. Openness is then *no longer* the basic character of φύσις as taken up in simple acknowledgment, the φύσις which makes it possible for τέχνη to grasp beings as such. Openness is also *not only* the condition of the possibility of the correctness of an assertion. As such a condition, it appears merely at first and preliminarily in the field of view of the critical return from correctness. After what we have experienced about the necessity of the question of truth, this cannot be the original access to the essence of truth. That access must proceed out of our need, our distress, out of the abandonment of beings by Being, while we take it seriously that Being is withdrawing from beings, whereby beings degenerate into mere objects of human contrivance and lived experience. What if this withdrawal itself belonged to the essence of Being? What if this were the still unrecognized truth, never to be experienced or expressed, of the whole metaphysics of the West: namely, that Being is in its essence self-concealing? What if the openness were first and foremost the clearing in the midst of beings, in which clearing the self-concealment of Being would be manifest? However it may be with the "answer" to this, the question of truth is not one we can decide by ourselves and in relation to ourselves precisely as neutral spectators. It is rather the question that will one day or another betray itself as the question of who we ourselves are.

In our retrospective sketch of the beginning of Western thinking, we said that man will be determined primordially as the custodian of the unconcealedness of beings. In the progression away from the beginning, man became the *animal rationale*. In the transition out of the first end of Western thinking into its other beginning, there has to be questioned, in a *still higher* necessity, with the carrying out of the question of truth, the question of who we are. This question will point in the direction of the possibility of whether man is not only the preserver of unconcealed beings but is precisely the custodian of the openness of Being. Only if we know that we do not yet know who we are do we ground the one and only ground which may release the future of a simple, essential existence [*Dasein*] of historical man from itself.

This ground is the essence of truth. This essence must be prepared in thought in the transition to another beginning. For the future, the situation of the powers which ground truth in the first place, namely poetry (and consequently art in general) and thinking, will be quite different than it was in the first beginning. Poetry will not be first, but in the transition the forerunner will have to be thinking. Art, however, will be for the future the putting into work of truth (or it will be nothing), i.e., it will be *one* essential grounding of the essence of truth. According to this highest standard, anything that would present itself as art must be measured as a way of letting truth come into being in these beings, which, as works, enchantingly transport man into the intimacy of Being while imposing on him the luminosity of the unconcealed and disposing him and determining him to be the custodian of the truth of Being.

APPENDICES

THE QUESTION OF TRUTH

I. Foundational issues in the question of truth.
II. Leaping ahead into the essentialization [*die Wesung*] of truth.
III. Recollection of the first shining forth of the essence of truth, ἀλήθεια (unconcealedness), as the basic character of beings. (The history of its flaming up and expiring from Anaximander to Aristotle.)
IV. The question of truth as the unfolding of the essentialization of Being, which comes to pass as the clearing of the "in the midst" of beings.
V. The question of truth as the grounding of ex-istence [*Da-sein*].
VI. The essentialization of truth as the truth of Being in the abyss.
VII. The abyss as the space of play of time. (Space and time in the previous interpretation, one determined by metaphysics and its guiding question).
VIII. The abyss and the strife. (*Da-sein*: earth and world).
IX. Truth and its shelter in beings as the recasting of beings into Being.
X. The full essentialization of truth and the inclusion of correctness.

Preview of the context for the discussion of I:

In I., *Da-sein* can only be kept in silence, because in *Da-sein*, *as* occurring through Being, the ground of truth is grounded, such that this ground becomes an abyss.

Here *Da-sein* cannot even be mentioned, because it would immediately be interpreted as an object and the determination of the essence of truth would be denigrated into a mere "new" theory. Instead of that, we attempted to show the necessity of the question of truth out of its necessary lack of being questioned in the first beginning. But this leads to the question of the primordial need and its basic disposition. And all this can be said only if *Da-sein* is already and steadily intended as the ground of the clearing for the self-concealing.

Everything will be misinterpreted if taken in terms of lived experience. Thoughtful reflection on the essence of truth as the clearing of Being can only be preparatory, but this is a necessary preparation.

The overthrow can only be accomplished by an art compelled by the most distant god, provided art is the putting into work of the truth.

FROM THE FIRST DRAFT

I. Foundational issues in the question of truth.

1. *The compelling power of the need arising from the abandonment by Being; terror as the basic disposition of the other beginning.*

It is transformed into mere curiosity within what is accessible to everyone. Philosophy is still "done," because it was once supposed to belong to the assets of culture, and caring for culture would presumably impede barbarism. The primordial questioning knowledge and the holding firm before the concealed have been replaced by a domination over everything, since everything has become obvious. That first luminosity of wonder, which had knowledge only of the darkness, has become the transparency of all knowing and doing, accessible to everyone and satisfying everyone.

Beings are—that is not worth a question, indeed it is not even worth mentioning. And to say what beings are, precisely *as* beings, is empty talk. For everyone knows what "Being" means, especially since it is the most general and most empty determination of everything. In this wasteland of utter indifference, what in the beginning produced the highest wonder has been lost—and the fact that here and there academic philosophy is still done diligently does not refute this loss but corroborates it.

There are only a very few who in the course of this history of the dissolution of the beginning have remained awake and surmise what has transpired. Insofar as they are still compelled to question, the compelling need must change in form and must be more undetermined, since the uniqueness of the first wonder has been lost and the subsequent tradition of questioning and thinking has forced itself in. What need compelled Kant to the Critique? What need compelled Hegel to the system of absolute knowledge? After even this questioning was abandoned and everything was left to calculating experience, slowly and in certain places something like the imminent irrelevance and meaninglessness of all beings flared up. And when an attempt was ventured to think anew (Nietzsche),[1] starting from an admission of this irrelevance, the former

1. Cf. Winter semester 1936-37 and Summer semester 1937. [I.e., *Nietzsche: Der Wille zur Macht als Kunst, GA, Bd.* 43, and *Nietzsches metaphysische Grundstellung im abendländischen Denken: Die Lehre von der ewigen Wiederkehr des Gleichen, GA, Bd.* 44—Tr.]

greatness of thought, then it became clear that the beginning had turned into the end and that the need and its compelling had to become different, assuming that there is still supposed to be another beginning.

After Nietzsche, and in a certain way through him (for as truly as he is the end, he is at the same time a transition), the other need comes into play, and this again only, as in the case of the first beginning, for a few rare persons, to whom is meted out the power to question and the power over declining in the transition.

The other need, that is, if we may say so, *our* need, has this peculiarity that it is not experienced as a need. Everything has become calculable, and consequently everything is understandable. There are no longer any limits to our domination over beings, if only our will is great enough and constant enough. Everything becomes obvious, without any impenetrable depths, and this transparency derives from a luminosity in which the eye of knowledge is dazzled to the verge of blindness.

Questioning, at one time the primordial eruption into the open on the part of what is concealed, and the pride in holding fast to what is worthy of questioning now succumb to the suspicion of weakness and insecurity. Questioning is a sign of a lack of the power to act. Whoever acknowledges and experiences this situation, one that has been becoming more acute for decades in the most varied forms, will find that beings are now taken for all that is, as if there were no such thing as Being and the truth of Being. Beings strut as beings and yet are abandoned by Being. The nearly unacknowledged need arising from the abandonment by Being becomes compelling in the basic disposition of terror. One can no longer be struck by the miracle of beings: that they are. For, quite to the contrary, this has become obvious long ago. And it is a gaping abyss that beings, apparently closer to reality than ever before, can be taken for all that is, while Being and the truth of Being are forgotten.

In wonder, the basic disposition of the first beginning, beings first come to stand in their form. Terror, the basic disposition of the other beginning, reveals behind all progress and all domination over beings a dark emptiness of irrelevance and a shrinking back in face of the first and last decisions.

2. *The question of the essence of truth as the necessity of the highest need arising from the abandonment of Being.*

It would be a very extrinsic conception of these various basic dispositions if we would see in wonder only inflamed desire and jubilation and seek terror in the nebulous realm of aversion, grief, and despair. Just as wonder bears in itself its own sort of terror, so does terror involve its own mode of self-composure, calm steadfastness, and new wonder. The quite different question, into which the basic disposition of terror compels, concerns the abandonment by Being and the fact that beings can *be* while the truth of Being remains forgotten. It asks whether this abysmal state of affairs does not belong to beings themselves, and whether now, after this experience with beings has been endured, the moment does not arrive to raise the question of beings again and indeed in a quite different manner. This other question determines the epoch of an other beginning. This other question can no longer, just as in the case of the first dawn of the day of beings, turn to beings in order then, in face of them, to ask what it means that beings are. The other question proceeds from terror before the groundlessness of beings: that no ground has been laid for them, indeed that grounding itself is held to be superfluous. This terror becomes aware that truths are still claimed and yet no one any longer knows or questions what truth itself is and how truth might belong to beings as such, something that can be asked and decided only if beings as beings have not fallen into oblivion with regard to their Being. Where, on the contrary, beings as beings have become obvious (and consequently the question of Being is merely a pursuit of "ontology" as a fixed discipline), then no one thinks to ask how beings as beings come into the open and what this opening might be, and how it takes place, such that the usual representations can conform to appearing beings. The absence of the question of the essence of truth becomes the strongest support for the obviousness of beings. The abandonment by Being is consoled by the absence of the question of truth, without, however, experiencing what bestows on it this consolation of the obvious.

If the abandonment by Being produces the highest need, which emerges as compelling in terror, then the question of the essence of what is true, the question of truth, proves to be the necessity of this need, what has to be surmounted first, precisely before the proper experience of the abandonment by Being. The truth itself—its essentialization—is the first and highest truth, in which alone all further truths, i.e., the founded relation to beings themselves, can find their ground.

Thus when we raise the question of truth, our motive is not a petty and fortuitous desire to critique and reform the traditional concept of truth. On the contrary, we are compelled by the most hidden and consequently the deepest need of the age, and by that alone.

3. *The question of truth and the question of Being.*

a) The unfolding of the question of truth as a reflection on the first beginning. The re-opening of the first beginning for the sake of another beginning.

Similarly, if the unfolding of the question of truth leads us to the history of truth, that does not happen from some sort of historiographical interest, one desirous of information about how things were in the past and how the present is rooted therein. On the contrary, the need arising from the abandonment by Being is the distress that the first beginning can no longer be mastered. This beginning is not something bygone but is, in the form of the end of the history which has declined from it, more contemporary and more pressing than ever, though also more concealed. If the question of truth is needed out of the deepest distress over the abandonment by Being in our age, then conversely the asking of this question has to articulate that need and in order to overcome it must first make sure that this need no longer remains extrinsic as the need arising from the lack of need, which is the form adopted by the most uncanny—namely the semblance of obviousness. The opening of the need, in which the beginning still dwells in the form of its excess, turns thereby into a reflection on the *first beginning* itself. This reflection must show that the first beginning, in its uniqueness, can never be repeated in the sense of a mere imitation, and that, on the other hand, it remains the only thing repeatable in the sense of a reopening of that by which the discussion has to commence if a beginning, and consequently the *other beginning*, is to come to be historically. The other beginning is not something withdrawn from the first beginning and from its history—as if the first beginning could cast the bygone behind itself—but precisely as the other beginning it is essentially related to the first, and only, beginning. This occurs, however, in such a way that in the other beginning the first is experienced more originally and is restored to its greatness. Afterward, through the domination of what succeeded it, still feeds upon it, and at the same time is declined from it, the first beginning was falsified into the "primitive," something that could not attain the height of the development and progress of what came later.

The need of the first beginning has its own form, and as a consequence wonder is there the compelling basic disposition, and the primordial and lasting question is there the question of beings: what are beings? On the other hand, the need of the other beginning has the form of an abandonment by Being, to which corresponds the basic disposition of terror. Therefore even the primordial question is different in the other beginning: the question of truth, the question of the essentialization of truth.

b) The question of truth as a preliminary question on behalf of the basic question of Being.

Truth, however, is the truth of Being, and therefore the question of truth is basically a preliminary question on behalf of the basic question of Being—the genuine question of *Being* in distinction to the previous question of *beings* as the guiding question in the history of the first beginning. (Cf. the first unfolding of this question in *Being and Time*. The question of the "meaning" of Being. Meaning = region of projection, the open ground of Being itself and of its essentialization. When, by comparison, Nietzsche happens to say that we must first know what "Being" is, what he means is precisely beings, and he is moving within the confusion of beings and Being, a confusion still rampant today. The reason for this aberration, however, resides not only in the fact that the basic question has been passed over, but the old guiding question that has been raised for centuries has not been unfolded as a question and thus is unknown in its own conditions.)

These foundational reflections on the question of truth and its necessity will have to make plain what is at stake in them. It should at least now be clear that here the question of truth is no longer a "problem of logic." All areas of sclerotic, and therefore only semblant, questioning have no need or necessity. All extrinsic attempts to found a new science now appear very traditional and flat—even prescinding from the fact that the question of truth can not at all be founded sufficiently by science, since every science, especially modern science, is a remote perversion of a definite kind of knowledge which has already decided on the essence and the type of truth normative for it (certitude).

II. Leaping ahead into the essentialization of truth.

4. *The question of the essentialization of truth as a question that founds history originally.*

The question of truth, as was clarified above, originates from the innermost need of our history and is the most genuine necessity of the work of founding history. History does not mean for us here the simple gathering of everyday public events, and a fortiori it is not such events as bygone. All of that certainly belongs to history and yet by no means touches its essence. For history is the occurrence in which, through man, beings become "more being." This occurrence involves most intrinsically the coming forth of beings as such into an openness which for its part requires a grounding and shelter in beings. This occurrence of the opening up of beings is, however, the essentialization of truth itself. Examined in its origin and thought with regard to its future, truth has the longest history because with it, following the character of its essentialization, history begins and ends. The question of the essentialization of truth is therefore the originally historical question, the question that grounds history, and is therefore historically different according to the respective historical moment.

We understand or, to put it more prudently, we surmise that our historical moment is that of the preparation for the other beginning. Yet this latter may also—since every beginning is decisive to the highest degree—be the final end. If this possibility did not exist, the beginning and its preparation would lose all trenchancy and uniqueness. The question of the essence of truth, as the primordial question of the other beginning, is different from that determination of the essence of truth which throughout the history of the first beginning could not be made primordially but only *ex post facto*.

In every case, however, the determination of the essence is apparently arbitrary, and so little can it be derived from what is given, that it is, on the contrary, the determinateness of the essence which first allows us to grasp a given something as this and not that. And if what is at stake is not only to represent (ἰδέα) the essence as whatness but to experience the essentialization, the *more original* unity of the what and the how, then this does not mean that the how would now be represented in addition to the what. We speak here about the experience of the essentialization and mean the conscious, willful, and affective entrance into the essence, in order to stand in it and to withstand it.

5. *Indication of the essentialization of truth through critical reflection and historical recollection.*

a) Preparation for the leap by securing the approach run and by predelineating the direction of the leap. Correctness as the start of the approach run, openness as the direction of the leap.

Now if even the representation of the essence (ἰδέα) cannot but appear arbitrary and groundless, yet on the other hand is constantly carried out without any strangeness, then this two-foldness will apply all the more to our entrance into the essentialization. Access to the essence always has about it something of the immediate and partakes of the creative, the freely arisen. We therefore speak of a leap, a leap ahead into the essentialization of truth. Admittedly, this terminology does not at first contribute a great deal toward the clarification or justification of our procedure. But it does suggest that this procedure must in every case be carried out by the individual expressly for himself. Whoever does not take this leap will never experience what it opens up. Speaking of a "leap" is also meant to intimate, however, that a preparation is still possible and necessary here: the securing of the approach run for the leap and the predelineation of its direction.

The question of truth, which we can and must raise, no longer dwells in its primordial state. Instead, there is behind it a rich tradition, one that has come down to the obvious representation of truth as correctness. We already know, or at all events believe we know, what truth is. Thereby we possess a starting point for the approach run to the leap into the more original essence of truth. In what sense this is the case was already clarified in the first discussions. The reflection on what correctness genuinely is, and would be, leads us to that which makes it possible in the first place and is the ground of this possibility. For a representation to be able to conform to beings as normative, the beings must, *prior* to this conformity and on behalf of it, show themselves to it and thus already stand in the open. The path or relation to beings must also be open, and on it the conforming and correct representation will move and will remain. Finally and above all, what must stand in the open is that which the representation carries out in order to present to itself the represented and to let the appearing beings show themselves. Correctness is what characterizes the conformity to . . . , and the latter must be able to move in an openness, indeed in that openness wherein there must be opened up that to which the representing conforms as well as the representing itself in its representation of the object. This open region and its openness constitute the ground of the possibility of the correctness of a representation. Consequently, if we take the usual determination of truth as correctness as the starting point of the approach run for the leap into our question of truth, then we may at the same time find therein an indication of the direction of the leap. The task is to leap into this open region itself and into its openness. The essentialization of this openness must be the essence of the truth, no matter how undeterminate and undeveloped it might now appear to us.

b) The experience of openness as unconcealedness (ἀλήθεια) in the first beginning. The unquestioned character of unconcealedness and the task of a more original experience of its essence on the basis of our need.

The start of our more original question is the determination of truth as correctness. We know, however, that this determination is an old one; it was reached in Greek philosophy—by Plato and above all by Aristotle. Now if correctness bears in itself openness as its ground and, as it were, oscillates in it, and consequently cannot be grasped without reference to it, then along with the positing of the determination of truth as correctness must not this openness also have been experienced? That is indeed the case. The simplest evidence is provided by the word the Greeks used in the beginning to name what we call "truth": ἀλήθεια, unconcealedness. The unconcealed stands and resides in the open. Hence the thinkers of the first beginning have also already experienced the original essence of truth and have thought it in advance, and so we have no reason to question more originally; indeed that would not even be possible.

To be sure, a distinction has to be made here. It is beyond discussion that the Greek thinkers experienced the unconcealedness of beings. But it is also undeniable that they did not make unconcealedness itself a question, nor was it unfolded in its essence and brought upon its ground. Instead, this experience of ἀλήθεια got lost. The proof for this unique occurrence within the great Greek philosophy is the fact that when it was imperative to raise the essence of truth to knowledge, ἀλήθεια became ὁμοίωσις (correctness). Nevertheless a last echo of the original essence of truth was always retained, without at all being able to prevail in the subsequent history of philosophy (cf. Aristotle, *Met.* Θ 10).

All the more pressing, then, is our task of experiencing this original essence of truth explicitly and grounding it. The historical necessity of the question of truth thus becomes surreptitiously richer in compelling power, and the more original essence of truth as openness loses more and more its apparent arbitrariness. For reflection on the ground of the possibility of correctness, as well as the recollection of the origin of the determination of truth as ὁμοίωσις, both led us to this dark and free-floating openness itself, unconcealedness.

At the same time it is clear that the mere change of name, speaking of "unconcealedness" instead of "truth," gains us nothing, even if we were to attempt what is intrinsically impossible, namely to rejuvenate the primordial Greek experiences from which this word arose, a word that, at the same time, first allowed these experiences to be experienced. Indeed it is certain that the essence of truth shone to the Greeks as ἀλήθεια; and it is equally certain that the Greek thinkers not only were incapable of mastering this essence of truth in their thinking but did not even put it into question. For Greek Dasein, ἀλήθεια remained the most powerful and at the same time the most hidden.

That the Greek thinkers did not raise the question of the essence and the ground of ἀλήθεια itself is not due to an incapacity of their thinking but, on the contrary, derives from the overpowering force of the primordial task: to speak for the first time of beings themselves as such.

If we now have to raise the question of truth in a more original way, that does not mean we may boast of a superiority. On the contrary. But just as little does it mean that the task is simply to supply a fitting definition of the ἀλήθεια which for the Greeks remained unquestioned and without further determination. Instead, notwithstanding all original adherence to the tradition, the task is to experience the essence of truth more originally *on the basis of our need* and to raise it to knowledge.

6. *The abandonment by Being as the need arising from the lack of need. The experience of the abandonment of beings by Being as need in the coming to light of the belongingness of Being to beings and the distinction of Being from beings.*

Our need is so deeply rooted that it is not felt by everyone. This lack of need is the most striking character of the unique need long ago prepared in history. Because this need is not felt by everyone, every reference to it is at first unintelligible or at least readily prone to misinterpretation. We have already spoken of the need arising from the "abandonment by Being." We clarified this designation by saying that historical man deals with, uses, and changes beings, and thereby experiences himself as a being—and the Being of beings does not concern him, as if it were the most indifferent. As progress and success show, one can certainly dispense with Being. Being will then once in a while, as the last remnant of a shadow, haunt mere representations, ones turned away from doing and acting and therefore already unreal. If this Being, compared to hefty and immediately pressing beings, is so negative and keeps its distance from experience and calculation and therefore is dispensable, then this cannot at all be called abandonment by Being. For abandonment exists only where what belongs indispensably has been withdrawn.

As soon as we speak of the abandonment by Being, we tacitly admit that Being belongs to beings and has to belong to beings in order for beings to be beings and for man to be a being in the midst of beings. The abandonment of beings by Being is therefore experienced as giving rise to need as soon as the belonging of Being to beings shines forth and the mere fussing with beings becomes questionable. But then, it would appear, the need is also already overcome, or at least the first step to overcome it has been taken. No. The need has then merely developed to a degree of acuteness that renders a decision, indeed *the* decision, inevitable: *either*, despite the shining forth of the belonging of Being to beings, the question of Being is dismissed and instead the fussing with beings is enhanced to gigantic proportions, *or* that terror we spoke of gains power and space and from then on no longer allows the belonging of Being to beings to be forgotten and takes as questionable all mere fussing over beings. The lack of need is precisely indifference over this decision.

Whether we are really questioning on the basis of need, and hence necessarily, in raising the question of truth and whether and how we thereby must already have traversed this decision and how a decisiveness lies behind our questioning, all that cannot be demonstrated in advance—indeed it cannot be demonstrated at all in the usual sense but can only be experienced in the course of reflection. If the question of truth, as we are putting it in train, is supposed to be nothing else than primordial reflection on Being itself, then there would at least be the possibility that we are questioning compelled by this need and that consequently the leaping ahead can become an impetus to true reflection. For where all roads are trodden and nothing more is left that could pass as inaccessible, it is already a step toward reflection to learn that something worthy of questioning has remained unquestioned.

This renewed reference to the enigmatic need arising from the lack of need should make clear to us that even if we could question on the basis of this need and enjoy the privilege of being allowed to question in such a way, yet at first and for the most part it would still appear that here, as elsewhere, we were merely dissecting words and concepts and were fabricating empty theories, perhaps ones even more intricate and bizarre. But this too belongs to the enduring of the need arising from the lack of need, namely that this appearance be taken over as inevitable.

7. *Directive sketch of the essence of truth on the basis of the need arising from the abandonment by Being.*

But how are we now supposed to set in motion the leap ahead into the essentialization of truth? "Leap ahead" is ambiguous: on the one hand, it means that a sketch of the approach run of the genuine leap and of its direction would be given in advance, and on the other hand it means that in all this an exemplary prior exercise of the leap has already been performed. At the beginning of this leaping ahead we know two things: (1) critical reflection and historical recollection direct us to the essentialization of truth as the openness of beings; (2) we attain the essentialization of the truth only by a leap, in virtue of which we come to stand in the essentialization, which is not the same as thinking a concept of the essence of truth under the guidance of a definition.

We will initially carry out the leap ahead as a directive sketch of the "essence" of truth on the basis of the need arising from the abandonment by Being. Even if we do not actually experience this and remain insensitive to it, we can still gain in a roundabout fashion an initial knowledge of what comes to pass in it.

a) Openness as the clearing for the vacillating self-concealment. Vacillating self-concealment as a first designation of Being itself.

We are always comporting ourselves to beings—actual, possible, and necessary. We ourselves, as beings, belong in this circuit of beings. Beings as a whole are known and familiar to us in a definite way; even where we do not turn to beings explicitly, they lie before us and surround us as accessible. We shall now deliberately attend to this obvious state of affairs that goes unnoticed in our everyday dealings. In so doing, we shall put aside all the theories and doctrines which might suggest themselves and which presumably have this state of affairs in view in some manner or other: e.g., that we are conscious of objects, that a subject, and several subjects together, relate to objects, etc. We shall now attend only to what precedes all that, and our directive shall be that beings—and we ourselves in their midst—lie in a certain sense open. In beings, such an openness holds sway. Our first and only effort shall be to draw close to this openness, without falling prey to the temptation to explain it prematurely, after scarcely perceiving it in the roughest manner.

In this openness, beings are familiar to us and known in different ways according to their different regions. Beings stand in a luminosity of knowledge and of sovereignty and afford ways and paths of penetration for the most diverse ways of being elaborated, formed, and considered. In every case, beings thereby prove to be independent and grounded in themselves. Beings dwell in a luminosity and provide, in very different degrees, free access to their autonomy. We may determine this closer and recapitulate by saying that beings stand in a luminosity, in a light, and allow free access and entrance—they are lighted. We speak of a clearing in the woods, a free luminous place. The openness of beings is such a clearing.

But at the same time beings are placed differently, and indeed not only by a being that is not accessible to us, and perhaps never will be, but by something concealed which conceals itself precisely when we immerse ourselves in the clearing, submit to the open beings, and are lost to them. That is exactly when we heed the least and are most rarely touched by the fact that these beings dwelling in the open "are"—or, as we say, "have" a Being. This latter, by which beings are distinguished from non-being, and owing to which they are and are such and such, does not stand in the clearing but in hiddenness. Consequently, the attempt to grasp this Being as if it were a being yields emptiness. Being is not merely hidden; it withdraws and conceals itself. From this we derive an essential insight: the clearing, in which beings are, is not simply bounded and delimited by something hidden but by something self-concealing.

Now, however, if Being is decisive for beings, and knowingly or not presses all activity and development of beings, beings we ourselves are not and ones we ourselves are, toward the Being of beings, toward what and how they are, then the clearing not only proves to be delimited by the self-concealing but is *for* the self-concealing. We can and even must understand this determination of the self-concealing—seen in terms of the clearing of beings—as a first essential designation of Being itself.

Since beings, and what is known as beings, stand in the clearing, Being reveals itself in a particular way. Its self-concealment is therefore one primordially proper to it. It shows itself and withdraws at the same time. This vacillating self-refusal is what is properly lighted up in the clearing, and yet for the most part it goes unheeded—corresponding to our comportment in the midst of beings. E.g., if we stand in a clearing in the woods, we see only what can be found within it: the free place, the trees about—and precisely not the luminosity of the clearing itself. As little as the openness is simply the unconcealedness of beings, but is the clearing *for* the self-concealing, so little is this self-concealment a mere being-absent. It is rather a vacillating, hesitant refusal.

In our recollection and critical deliberation we found that the ground of the possibility of "correctness" as the usual concept of truth lies in an openness of beings, and that this openness was already experienced in the beginning and was named ἀλήθεια. This openness of beings has now shown itself to be the clearing for the vacillating self-concealment, which constantly points into the clearing. Accordingly,[1] truth is not simply the unconcealedness of beings— ἀλήθεια—but, more originally understood, is the clearing for the vacillating self-concealment. The name "vacillating self-concealment" is a name for Being itself, and, by the most preliminary allusion, it implies that the essence of truth is in the most intimate way related to Being itself, so intimately that perhaps Being itself is in need of truth for its own most proper essentialization, and truth is not a mere supplement to it.

b) The clearing for self-concealment as the supporting ground of humanity. Man's grounding of this supporting ground as *Da-sein*.

An essential step is still outstanding, a step that belongs intrinsically to the fulfillment of this preliminary directive sketch of the essence of truth. We first characterized truth as the openness of beings (unconcealedness). It might appear that the further determination of truth in terms of the concealedness inherent in it was merely an ancillary representation on our part. But the clearing is the clearing for the self-concealing, and, above all, the clearing of beings is not something we ourselves merely think or represent. On the contrary, it is something in which we ourselves stand and apparently nothing of our own doing. We stand in this clearing in such a way that it first opens for us a relation to beings—and to ourselves as well. It is the supporting ground of our humanity, insofar as this is essentially determined through the distinctive ability to relate to beings as such and hence to be determined by beings as such. But the clearing of beings is this supporting ground only insofar as it is the clearing for the vacillating self-concealment, for the entrance of Being itself into what is lighted up. On the other hand, it also holds that if man would not be, then neither could this clearing come to pass. The clearing for the self-concealing—truth—is the supporting ground of humanity, and humanity comes to pass only by grounding and being exposed to the supporting ground as such. While man stands as a being in the openness of beings, he must also at the same time stand in a relation to what is self-concealing. The ground of humanity must therefore be grounded *through* humanity as ground.

Thus, if we would understand the essence of truth in its essentialization, we will have to see that a representation of the correctness of knowledge is not sufficient—indeed, even further, that a representation will never attain the essentialization of truth. For truth as the clearing for the self-concealing is the *ground* of humanity—something other than we ourselves are, and to which we nevertheless belong and must belong, if we propose to know truth originally. Thus the essentialization of truth will be attained only if the usual everyday way of being human is successfully dislocated, as it were,

1. [Reading *demnach* for *dennoch*, following the second edition.—Tr.]

and is then allowed to settle on its proper ground. Hence the need of the leap, which we can now prepare only as regards its direction.

Truth, however, is grounded as the ground through that which we call *Da-sein*, that which sustains man and is entrusted to him only rarely, as both donation and destiny, and only to those among men who are creative and are grounding. The "*Da*" [the "there"] refers to that clearing in which beings stand as a whole, in such a way that in this "*Da*" the Being [*Sein*] of open beings shows itself and at the same time withdraws. To be this "*Da*" is a destiny of man, in correspondence to which he grounds that which is itself the ground of the highest possibilities of his Being.

Ever since man has comported himself to beings as such and formed himself as a being on the basis of this relation, ever since man has been historical, the clearing for the self-concealing must have come to pass. Which does not imply that since then this ground of historical humanity was experienced as ground and was grounded. It was not by accident that this ground was surmised within the Greeks' experience of what they called ἀλήθεια. But very soon, and again not accidentally, it was misinterpreted and forced into oblivion. The representation of man was itself not determined originally, on the basis of his most original essence, because that has remained concealed up to this very hour: namely, that *man is the being which, in the midst of beings, bears the truth of Being*. Instead, the concept of man was constructed with reference to animals and living things in general, i.e., with reference to something other than man himself. Man was distinguished from the animal only insofar as he was declared to be the "rational animal," a determination which is still, in different variations, powerful and respectable today. And this non-original determination of man is now also supposed to represent the ground for the interpretation of everything proper to man as man—his knowledge and his creations, his self-surpassing and his self-destruction. The ground of humanity and thereby the essence of truth thus remain hidden in their full essentialization.

It is as if the most extreme need into which man was pressed historically—the need arising from the lack of need, the pursuit of truths without a relation to truth itself—it is as if this need had to compel him now to reflect on the ground of his essence. And should we then be surprised if this ground—supposing we could look into it—would open itself up for us precisely as an abyss, since we still live all too much on the basis of the habits of a previous age and take the usual and the obvious for the essence?

c) The question of truth, and the dislocation of humanity out of its previous homelessness into the ground of its essence, in order for man to become the founder and the preserver of the truth of Being.

As inexorably as genuine questioning throws us back entirely upon ourselves and will tolerate no dissent, and as certain as history is grounded only in the overcoming of the historiographical, that is how little we can detach ourselves from all previous history and place ourselves, as it were, in a void.

We must insist over and over that what is at stake in the question of truth as raised here is not simply an alteration of the previous concept of truth, nor a supplementation of the usual representation, but a transformation of humanity itself. This transformation is not the result of new psychological or biological insights. For man is not here the object of any sort of anthropology. On the contrary, man is here in question in the most profound and the most extensive respect, the one properly foundational; i.e., we are questioning man in his relation to Being, or, after the turning, we are questioning Being and its truth in relation to man. The determination of the essence of truth is accompanied by a necessary transformation of man. Both are the same. This transformation signifies the dislocation of humanity out of its previous home—or, better, from its homelessness—into the ground of its essence, in order for man to become the founder and the preserver of the truth of Being, to be the "there," as the ground employed by the essence of Being itself.

The dislocation of humanity—to be this ground—turns man away from himself the furthest and into a relation to Being itself. But only out of this furthest distance can man truly find himself back, i.e., be who he is.

We have been speaking of "man," expressing ourselves as concisely as possible. But the man that concerns us is historical man, which means the one who creates history, is sustained by history, and is beset by history. This historical man is not a separate "individual," dragging his past behind himself. Nor does it mean several individuals, belonging together in the form of a society. Individuation and society are themselves only possible and necessary modes of historical humanity and do not at all exhaust it. Historical man: that shall mean for us the unexhausted unique fullness of essential human possibilities and necessities, specifically—which is decisive here—ones arising from man's relation to the truth of Being itself. Questioning on the basis of such a pre-view, we would represent precisely the possibility of the beginning of an entirely different history, in which the destiny of the single individual as well as of society would be determined differently, so differently that the previous representations could no longer suffice.

Thus the dislocation of man back into his ground has to be carried out in the first place by those few, solitary, and uncanny ones, who in various ways as poets, thinkers, as builders and artists, as doers and actors, ground and shelter the truth of Being in beings through the transformation of beings. Through the rigor of the decisions which lie ahead, they become, each in his way and unknown to the many, a silent sacrifice.

If we appraise the reflection on this dislocation [*Verrückung*] of man from the standpoint of sound common sense and its predominance, we will reject it as deranged ["*verrückt*"], to play cleverly with a word, and will not even take the pains to reject such reflection but will simply ridicule it.

But this will not mislead ones who know, to the extent that there are any. For a case which has not yet been mastered is still in the air, the latest in the history of German thought, the case of Nietzsche. Fortunately, we have the incontrovertible fact that this thinker lapsed into madness. By means of this circumstance it is possible to ward off his most decisive meditation—the thought of the eternal recurrence of the same—in its totally strange character and in the inexorableness of its perspectives and questioning, by interpreting it as a precursor of madness and an offspring of despair. But what about that other one, still greater, whose poetry was further in advance, namely Hölderlin?

Have we at all considered sufficiently that something miraculous comes to pass whenever the history of the West, in its most profound meditations, surmises its unrolling to its end? The miracle is that the ones who suffered such meditation, and created it, and hence bore the knowledge of what was entirely other, were prematurely torn away from the sanity of their Dasein—and this in wholly different ways in their own respective domains: Schiller, Hölderlin, Kierkegaard, van Gogh, Nietzsche. Did they all merely "break down," as an extrinsic calculation would perhaps ascertain, or was a new song sung to them, one that never tolerates an "and so forth" but demands the sacrifice of the "shortest path" (Hölderlin)?

These names are like enigmatic signs, inscribed in the most hidden ground of our history. We hardly give a thought to the sheer power of this series of signs, which is not to say that we would be strong enough to understand it. These signs are harbingers of a change of history, lying deeper and reaching further than all "revolutions" within the compass of the activities of men, of peoples, and of their contrivances. Here something comes to pass, for which we have no measure and no space—at least not yet—and we therefore force it into disfiguration and disguise, if we speak about it by means of language as constituted hitherto.

So if we are pointing to it in our sketch of the question of truth, then that is only meant to indicate how far we are turned away from the real path of our history and how much there is need for even the most minor power to prepare ourselves and future ones to enter into this path once and for all. Such preparation requires, prior to all truths, that truth itself become a question and a necessity. Necessity arises only from original need. And this is exactly what we withdraw from the most when we steal away on the exits to the past.

d) The question of the essentialization of truth as the question of the essentialization of Being.

The question of truth is fundamentally the question of the openness for the self-concealing. And what, in an exceptional and unique sense, conceals itself in the domain of open beings is Being. We experience this in the most prosaic and yet most enigmatic event, namely that beings most immediately press upon us and impose themselves and that only beings seem to be. But perhaps our seeming to manage, in the domain of beings, with beings alone is the most uncanny semblance that plays with us, a semblance that certainly prevails constantly and erupts, but which can nevertheless be overcome. When we set forth on the path of the question of truth, we take pains to overcome this semblance to the effect that if beings are, then only beings are open. For openness is on behalf of self-concealment. And what conceals itself is Being. Insofar as self-concealment requires openness, this latter belongs as well to the essentialization of Being. The question of truth is the question of the essentialization of Being. Being, however, is that which needs man as the founder and preserver of its truth: man *as* this or that one, but not simply any man but only the one who bestows to truth its ground and home, and who bears the openness for the self-concealing, who *is* the "there" [*Da*]. That is how truth as the essentialization of Being comes to pass, founded in the *Da-sein* of man, between Being [*Sein*] and being-the-there [*Da-sein*].

Truth belongs to the essentialization of Being without exhausting its essence. Truth belongs to the appropriating event, and truth belongs to Being. That is why the Greeks experienced for the first time, in the thinking of beings as such, unconcealedness as the beingness of beings. But because they did not ask about Being itself, truth degenerated into correctness, became something for itself, and lost the essential relation to Being.

If we now recollect the traditional and ordinary conception of truth as correctness and consider that it was finally determined as a relation between subject and object, then we can recognize in the subject-object relation a very remote layer of that relation between Being and being-the-there, a layer entirely ignorant of its origin. The question about truth begins with this view in order to unfold for the first time its full bearing and to lose completely the character of an isolated question. Indeed still more: not only is it inserted into this most extreme and broadest realm of thoughtful knowledge in general, but the question of truth becomes at the same time, in terms of the approach we characterized, the first leap into the heart of the basic question of philosophy.

Therefore it should not be surprising that everything we say beyond the ordinary concept of truth will at first, and for a long time, seem very strange. Therefore we must all the more assure for ourselves what is already accessible in the tradition as an echo of the original essence of truth and which is expressed in the word ἀλήθεια (unconcealedness). In this way our question of truth will become historical in a double respect: on the one hand, insofar as there is prepared in it a transformation of humanity hitherto and its relation to beings (and consequently the "hitherto" necessarily enters into the discussion) and on the other hand, insofar as even the more original determination of the essence of truth already and by necessity appears in the knowledge of truth in the first beginning, without being explicitly mastered. Thus what our question needs for its justification and elucidation, and at the same time for the removal of the suspicion of arbitrariness, is an explicit carrying out of historical recollection. And only its actual execution will allow us to see the extent to which this is distinct from historiographical acquaintance with past opinions on truth.

III. Recollection of the first shining forth of the essence of truth as ἀλήθεια (unconcealedness).

8. *Recollection of the first knowledge of truth at the beginning of Western philosophy as an indication of the proper question of the more original essence of truth as openness.*

The recollection of the first knowledge of truth at the beginning of Western philosophy should serve to indicate what is announced in the essence of truth as openness regarding essential relations, even if there they are undetermined and ungrounded. The carrying out of this recollection is more difficult than might appear at first sight. What the Greeks thought about truth has been known for a long time and has been presented in a more or less full account ever since there has been historiographical research into the history of philosophy. Of course, these historiographical reports have been guided by the traditional concept of truth as correctness. Thus we discover what the Greeks said about truth in that sense, and we can observe how far they progressed in the unfolding of this concept of truth and to what extent they fell short. We find only what we seek, and in historiography we are seeking only what we may know in relation to the guiding concept of truth as correctness. We are thereby precisely not seeking unconcealedness.

To be at all able to carry out the recollection of the first shining forth of the essence of truth as ἀλήθεια, we ourselves must have already asked about the more original essence of truth as the openness of beings. We are thus moving in the well-known circle of all understanding and interpretation. Conversely, one could now say that if we have already inquired into the original essence of truth and consequently have at our command a knowledge of it, then it is superfluous to drag the past back in. Our foregoing considerations have already eliminated this objection and its very foundations. From now on it is to be noted that we can focus on the first shining forth of ἀλήθεια only if we ourselves at the same time, and above all, investigate the original essence. We will better see the essential the more decisive our questioning is and in that way encounters past history.

The carrying out of the recollection of the first shining forth of ἀλήθεια comes down to a discussion of the essential steps of the basic movement of the great Greek philosophy, whose beginning and end are attached to the names Anaximander and Aristotle. What later arises as so-called "Greek philosophy" has another character, no longer the original; what we then have are either scholastic trends in the wake of Plato and Aristotle, or practical-moral philosophies like those of the Stoa and Epicurus, or even attempts at a renaissance of the ancient Greek philosophy under the influence of Christian faith or the religious systems of later antiquity, renaissances which go by the name of Neoplatonism. Subsequently, all these "philosophies" became historically more influential than the genuine and originally great Greek philosophy. The ground of this fact resides in the linkage with Christianity. The great Greek philosophy fell more and more into oblivion, and when it was indeed sought out it was completely covered over. That Aristotle became the principal master of "philosophy" in the middle ages does not contradict this, for on the one hand what was called philosophy in medieval times was not philosophy but only a preamble of reason on behalf of theology, as required by faith. And, on the other hand, Aristotle was precisely therefore not understood in the Greek way, i.e., on the basis of the primordial thought and poetry of Greek Dasein, but in a medieval fashion, i.e., in an Arabic-Jewish-Christian way.

The first attempt at a philosophical reflection on the beginning of Western philosophy, and hence on the great philosophy of the Greeks, was carried out by Hegel on the basis of the system he himself elaborated. The second attempt, entirely different in direction and character, is the work of Nietzsche. Yet neither of these two attempts to restore the broken bond with the Greeks—employing a creative recollection to make essential for us what was essential for them, i.e., not merely imitating the Greeks or taking them over—is original enough, because they were not ignited or supported by *the* question, the one through which the primordial Greek thinking must surpass itself and enter into another beginning.

9. *Articulation of the historical recollection in five steps of reflection.*

The heart of this question is the question of truth as we have developed it. The carrying out of the recollection of the first shining forth of ἀλήθεια—in the sense of a discussion of the essential steps of the basic movement of the great Greek philosophy between Anaximander and Aristotle—is impossible within the framework of these lectures. To be sure, neither can we take as a substitute the extensive scholarly research of the historiography of philosophy. This research knows all the names and doctrines and writings and presents them time and again. It can draw all the lines of connection between the thinkers and all their dependencies on one another, but philosophy itself does not thereby make an appearance, for no real question is asked—and that is because, as ones who have come later, and specifically as people of today, we can claim to know better, and already do know everything much better, than these old thinkers did.

The recollection of the first shining forth of ἀλήθεια, as we require it and which we hold to be possible only on the basis of the question of truth, may be articulated in five levels of reflection:

1. The unexpressed flaming up of ἀλήθεια in the pronouncements of Anaximander.

2. The first unfoldings of ἀλήθεια, though not ones explicitly directed to a foundation, in Heraclitus, Parmenides, the tragic poets, and Pindar.

3. The last glimmering of ἀλήθεια within the question of beings (τί τὸ ὄν) as the basic philosophical question in Plato and Aristotle.

4. The extinguishing of ἀλήθεια and its transformation into ὁμοίωσις (correctness).

5. The mediate and mediated transition from ἀλήθεια to ὁμοίωσις on the by-way over incorrectness (falsity—ψεῦδος).

For the purpose of these lectures, we will follow only the middle of these five levels, the third, and even then only the last glimmering of ἀλήθεια in Plato. We will do so, of course, not in the mode of an empty survey of Platonic philosophy but by *participating* in Plato's philosophizing. All of his dialogues, indeed nearly every fragment of his dialogues, direct us mediately or immediately to the question of ἀλήθεια. We will choose, however, a pre-eminent fragment from a dialogue, which not only deals explicitly with ἀλήθεια, but also displays a pre-eminent character in the very way of dealing with it, insofar as Plato there, as we say, speaks in an "allegory."

SUPPLEMENT TO §40

Need (the need arising from the lack of need: the abandonment of beings by Being) determines the necessity (of the question of the truth of Being); the necessity determines the direction of the question (the question of the Being of truth) as a preliminary question and hence determines the content of truth, the sphere of its essence.

Truth: as overcoming the end, not correctness; as a transition to another beginning, not ἀλήθεια. And yet only "not"; but ἀλήθεια more originally as such: openness; the openness in itself: as it holds sway originally: *Da-sein*.

It is not the mere critical exposition of the prevailing concept of truth, but the necessity of the present need, that determines the essential approach to truth. Therefore that critical discussion—apparently coming from nowhere like a bolt from the blue—is already determined from the experienced necessity of the question of truth, which springs forth from the end of metaphysics to the beginning of the truth of Being (appropriating event).

The displacement, according to which man is *at once* posited both into the free space of the daring act of creating and into the unprotectedness of the perseverance of his dwelling. Both of these belong to the essence of the openness of the "in-between"; both become especially important in the question of how this openness as such is supposed to be grounded. But both are submerged, turned around, and distorted if, out of that dislocation into the primordial essence, man issues forth as the rational animal; and that is what actually happened.

SUPPLEMENT TO §41

Openness is not only the condition of the possibility of the correctness of an assertion. As such a condition it appears for the first time only in the subsequent critical reference. But to be such a condition does not exhaust the essence of openness, nor does it touch the heart of this essence. For openness expresses something even more original than ἀλήθεια, not only the unconcealedness of present beings, but also what is illuminated in the clearing and the clearing itself, in which an unconcealed being can stand forth in the first place.

What is this clearing in the midst of beings? What must it be, so that in it beings can encounter and belong to one another? Where is its ground and how does this illuminated "in the midst" come to presence, into which man is displaced by disposition and which he has to occupy and preserve in the forbearance of his creative activity? The openness of the illuminated "in-between," in which man comes to stand, reveals itself in this way as the ground of humanity itself—not of some sort of universal humanity, but of that man who by means of the question of the essence of truth as openness first raises the question of who he is. In our retrospective sketch of the beginning of Western thinking, we said that man was determined there as the custodian of the unconcealedness of beings and later declined into the rational animal. In asking about the more original essence of truth as the openness of beings, the question of who man is first attains its keen edge and its necessity. For this question now asks whether man really is the steward of the essence of truth and whether all his truths and correctnesses do not remain fragmentary and preliminary, as long as and as often as he forgets this stewardship.

The essence of openness is not exhausted there but is more original. That is the reference of what was said about disposition and its dislocating and casting asunder of beings.

Openness is not only what makes this possible—i.e., a particular human comportment, the predicating and judging about objects—but is what makes man himself possible in the first place, insofar as he is finally and genuinely understood in terms of that which his Western history primordially throws him into, in order that, as it seems, at first he would *not* grasp it but would only disfigure it by forgetting it.

And what is this? The fact that man is not only—as we interpreted him in our retrospective sketch—the preserver of the unconcealedness of beings but is the steward of the openness of Being itself, in whose play of space and time beings first come to be beings (more so and less). Then this would be the decision of future mankind and the preparation of the present, that man of today might overcome himself and his truth, and instead of continuing on, i.e., continuously treading in the same place, might find his essence out of a more original ground and begin to become that essence—namely, the guardian of the truth of Being.

Openness comes to pass as the clearing of self-concealment, as the "there" [*Da*] in the grounding-there [*Da-gründung*] of being-the-there [*Da-sein*].

EDITOR'S AFTERWORD

This volume, number 45 in the series, is the text of a lecture course Martin Heidegger presented one hour per week during the Winter semester 1937–1938 at the University of Freiburg. The course bore the same title as this book and is published here for the first time.

The editor had available Heidegger's own manuscript as well as two different typed transcriptions of it which Heidegger charged Fritz Heidegger [his brother] to prepare and a third typescript by Hildegard Feick. The manuscript at hand is in German script and presents the text of the lectures fully elaborated and formulated. The manuscript begins with pages a through d and then continues with sheets numbered 1 through 50; occasionally, a number is used for more than one page by virtue of a small letter added to it. The manuscript also includes the "recapitulations." These are on separate pages and are again fully elaborated and formulated. Heidegger annotated them with the page number of the manuscript to which they refer and inserted them himself in the appropriate places. The written text of the lectures and recapitulations proceeds without a break on the left-hand side of the page, and the writing is crosswise. Heidegger reserved the right side for supplements, corrections, and marginal remarks.

The second transcription by Fritz Heidegger followed the first after some time and is distinguished from the earlier by incorporating the emendations Heidegger had introduced into the manuscript. The first copy of this second transcription is extant in bound form, and, as the hand-signed dedication attests, Heidegger presented it to Vili Szilasi on his sixtieth birthday. The handwritten title page bears the motto: "Αὔη ψυχὴ σοφωτάτη καὶ ἀρίστη (Heraclitus 118): dispassionate soul—wisest and most noble." The typescript Heidegger instructed Hildegard Feick to prepare incorporates a number of his handwritten revisions of this gift copy for Wilhelm Szilasi.

The editor worked entirely within the framework marked out by the directives Heidegger himself gave for the proper preparation of his texts for publication. The transcriptions were checked several times both against the original manuscript and against one another. Some misreadings were discovered. Furthermore, beyond the first handwritten emendation of the manuscript, which was already incorporated into the second transcription of Fritz Heidegger, the manuscript of the lecture was reworked by Heidegger once again, this time more lightly and for the most part limited to matters of style, all in accord with the directives he himself conveyed to the editors of his writings. This revision was also incorporated into the present volume. In addition, the second transcription produced by Fritz Heidegger was also subject to a few minor handwritten corrections and a larger handwritten reworking of that part of the text which comprises §§36–38 of the present volume. This reworking, however, does not exceed the level of the reflection inherent in the lectures as delivered.

Since, on the whole, the manuscript of the lectures, including the recapitulations, contains no divisions, the text was subsequently articulated meaningfully into sections. Heidegger himself largely attended to the numbering of the sections; where necessary, this was revised and made uniform by the editor. The editor also deleted the epithets and interjections, characteristic of the lecture style but disturbing in a printed text, to the extent that they were not already stricken by Heidegger himself.

To present a detailed table of contents, the text was thoroughly articulated and titles were given to each segment. According to Heidegger's directive, such a table was to substitute for an index of names and subjects, something he did not at all want. The manuscript of the lecture contains only two titles: that of the present second chapter of the preparatory part as well as the title of the main part. The articulation of the text into preparatory and main parts, the further partition into chapters and sections, the division of the latter into subsections, and all the titles, with the exception of the two just mentioned, were the work of the editor. These titles were drawn exclusively from the words Heidegger himself employed in the respective segment.

The quotation marks surrounding many words correspond faithfully to their occurrence in the handwritten manuscript. In order not to interfere with the text by introducing an interpretation, Heidegger's distinctive way of writing "*Seyn*" [archaic form of

"*Sein*," "Being"] and "*Sein*" was also carried over from the manuscript, even where a correction might have suggested itself from the context.

The few footnotes in this volume derive without exception from Heidegger and were only supplemented bibliographically. In verifying the citations, Heidegger's own copies of the texts were consulted.

Page 81 of this volume contains a reference Heidegger inserted in the continuous text of the manuscript and put in parentheses: "(Unsaid: the passing of the last god. Cf.: *Vom Ereignis*)." He is referring here to his most comprehensive, still unpublished, treatise from the years 1936–1938, which he himself relegated to the third main division of his collected works. The "official title" of this manuscript—as Heidegger says at the beginning of the treatise—is *Beiträge zur Philosophie* ["Contributions to Philosophy"], but its "essential subtitle" is *Vom Ereignis* ["On the Appropriating Event"]. Ever since that treatise, "appropriating event" has been the guiding term of his thinking, as Heidegger notes in a marginal remark to his "Letter on humanism" (Cf. *Wegmarken*, *GA* 9, p. 316).

The first appendix of the present volume, "The question of truth"—inserted in the manuscript before the beginning of the main part—bears, near the title, the parenthetical remark, "Not to be delivered." The first draft of the lectures was providing for them to be worked out according to the ten divisions listed in that outline. This plan was stopped short and abandoned, and Heidegger decided to elaborate the main part of the lectures exclusively under the title which stands first in the outline, namely "Foundational issues in the question of truth." Pages 19–36 of the first draft are preserved, however, and they are printed here as the second appendix. This fragmentary text begins with the conclusion of division I and continues with the complete division II and the incomplete division III. This fragment, too, is fully elaborated and formulated in the manuscript and was included in Fritz Heidegger's first transcription. The articulation of the divisions into sections with arabic numerals and the formulation of the titles of these sections are the work of the editor. Both supplements, to §§40 and 41, were inserted as such by Heidegger into his handwritten manuscript and were included in both typescripts of Fritz Heidegger.

I owe great thanks to Hermann Heidegger, the administrator of his father's literary remains by the latter's own last will and testament, for his confidence, collaboration, and the generous dialogue which accompanied all my editorial work.

I also express my cordial thanks to Hartmut Tietjen for his helpful assistance in the preparation of this volume. I thank Luise Michaelsen for her very thorough and careful collaboration in reading the proofs. I thank Hans-Helmuth Gander for a large share of the proofreading as well as for faithful help in various stages of the work; the repeated comparison of the different texts fell to him. I also express my gratitude to Sonja Wolf, of the Freiburg Seminar for Classical Philology, for the final inspection of the page proofs.

Friedrich-Wilhelm von Herrmann
Freiburg i. Br., July 1984

AFTERWORD TO THE SECOND EDITION

This second edition has corrected the few typographical errors in the first.

Under the title, "From a discussion of the question of truth," Martin Heidegger published a slightly revised extract of the text of the present lecture course (printed here on pages 78–81) in a small almanac of Neske Publishers, on the occasion of their tenth anniversary (*Zehn Jahre Neske Verlag*. Pfullingen, 1962, pp. 19–23). The editor neglected to include this information in his afterword to the first edition and hereby makes up for that omission.

In his afterword to the first edition, (p. 191), the editor explained Heidegger's reference (on page 81 of the present volume) to the manuscript "*Vom Ereignis*" by alluding to the major work *Beiträge zur Philosophie*, which was at that time still unpublished. In the meanwhile, this manuscript has come out, marking the one hundredth anniversary of Heidegger's birth, as the third main division of his collected works (*Gesamtausgabe* Bd. 65). For more particulars on the special relation the present lecture course from the Winter semester 1937–1938 has to the *Beiträge zur Philosophie*, which was worked out between 1936 and 1938, see the editor's afterword to the latter volume, p. 513f.

Friedrich-Wilhelm von Herrmann
Freiburg i. Br., March 1992